Diving & Snorkeling

Trinidad & Tobago

Lawson Wood

D1052896

LONELY PLANET PUBLICATIONS
Melbourne • Oakland • London • Paris

Tobago

st edition
April, 2000

Published by
Lonely Planet Publications
192 Burwood Road, Hawthorn, Victoria 3122, Australia

Other offices
150 Linden Street, Oakland, California 94607, USA
10A Spring Place, London NW5 3BH, UK
1 rue du Dahomey, 75011 Paris, France

Photographs
by Lawson Wood, Michael Lawrence, Lesley Orson, Ned
Friary, Wolf Winter, Jim Stephens, Steve Simonsen, Steve
Rosenberg, Len Zell, and Jean Pierce & Kris Newman

Front cover photograph
Diver and giant brain coral at Kelleston Drain
by Lawson Wood

Back cover photographs
Hermit crab, by Lesley Orson
Diver and manta ray, by Michael Lawrence
Trinidad's Carnival, by Jim Stephens for TIDCO

Many of the images in this guide are available for
licensing from **Lonely Planet Images**
email: lpi@lonelyplanet.com.au

ISBN 0 86442 777 8

text & maps © Lonely Planet 2000
photographs © photographers as indicated 2000
dive site maps are Transverse Mercator projection

LONELY PLANET and the Lonely Planet logo are
trademarks of Lonely Planet Publications Pty Ltd.

Printed by H&Y Printing Ltd., Hong Kong

Contents

Author

Lawson Wood

A diver since 1963, Lawson Wood lives in the Borders of Scotland with his wife Lesley, who contributes greatly to the photography and research of his books. He is a Fellow of the Royal Geographical Society, Fellow of the Royal Photographic Society, founding member of the Marine Conservation Society and founder of the first marine reserve in Scotland. With more than 13,000 dives logged in all of the world's oceans, he has contibuted articles and photographs to publications worldwide, and is the author of several Pisces dive guides and other diving-related books.

LESLEY ORSON

From the Author

This book would have been impossible without the unswerving support of my wife Lesley—she is not only my dive buddy, she is an accomplished photographer and author in her own right. We had incredibly generous help and support from the Tourism and Industrial Development Company of Trinidad & Tobago (TIDCO). The people from the Ministry's London, Scarborough and Port of Spain offices were friendly, courteous and above all, enthusiastic. Special mention must go to Prime Minister Basdeo Panday, Neemah Persad, Sandra Hendrickson, Christine Taylor, Liz Lower and Anita at MKI for their help and logistical support. Robert Ward, Lea and Beth from Harlequin Worldwide Travel, British Airways, Caledonian Airways, British West Indian Airways (BWIA) and Air Caribbean for their support on national and international flights. Shaun Robinson, who first introduced us to Tobago diving and helped tremendously on this project. Gaylord Kelshall and the Chaguaramas Military History and Aviation Museum. Carol Peck and Tali from Tobago Dive Experience. Keith Darwent of Aquamarine Dive. Ricardo Nedd from R&C Diver's Den. Anne and Bjarne Olesen of Man Friday Diving. Ellis John and Scotty of Tobago Dive Masters. James Young of Dive Tobago. David Byrnes of Wild Turtle Dive Safari. Marco and Sharon de Priester of Proscuba Dive Center. A special thanks to Ricky Rampaul and his good buddy Solomon, who introduced us to the delights of diving in Trinidad. Manta Lodge; Blue Waters Inn; Rex Turtle Beach; Grafton Beach Resort; Arnos Vale Hotel; Sanctuary Villa Resort; Ian Lambie and the Asa Wright Nature Centre; Elton Puchet, In Joy Tours and the Silver Stars; Victor Nixon, our taxi driver and mentor on Tobago; Susan Shurland-Maharaj, Information Officer of the Institute of Marine Affairs; KJP of Edinburgh and Fuji, who supplied all of the film. Stahlsac. Eastern Visual Communications for all film processing; Sea & Sea of Paignton in Devon, England for all underwater camera equipment; The Shark Group of Amble in Northumberland, England for all other diving equipment.

Photography Notes

Lawson Wood's photographs were taken using Nikonos V, Nikon F-801 and Nikon F-90. Lenses used on the amphibious Nikonos system were 35mm, 28mm, 20mm, 15mm and 12mm (and varied extension tubes supplied by Ocean Optics in London). Lenses for the housed Nikons were 14mm, 55mm, 85mm, 60mm, 105mm, 35-70mm zoom. Tamron supplied 28-200mm zoom, 20-40mm zoom and 70-300mm zoom lenses. Housing manufacture is by Subal in Austria and Sea & Sea of Japan. YS120 duo, YS30 duo, YS50 and YS300 electronic flashes were used in virtually all of Lawson's underwater photographs; these were supplied by Sea & Sea Ltd. For the land cameras, the Nikon SB24 and SB26 were used. Additional lighting was supplied by Night Rider Technical Lighting System; all connectors were from Camera Tech in San Francisco. Film stock used was Fujichrome Velvia, Fujichrome Provia and Fujichrome RDP. Eastern Visual Communications in Edinburgh did all film processing.

Michael Lawrence contributed many of the images in this book. Others were provided by Lesley Orsen, Ned Friary, Wolf Winter, Jim Stephens, Steve Simonsen, Steve Rosenberg, Len Zell, and Jean Pierce & Kris Newman. Images by Wolf Winter and Jim Stephens were provided courtesy of TIDCO.

From the Publisher

This first edition was produced in Lonely Planet's U.S. office under direction from Roslyn Bullas, the Pisces Books publishing manager. Wendy Smith edited the book with invaluable contributions from Sarah Hubbard and Senior Editor Debra Miller, and proofreading from Paige R. Penland. Emily Douglas designed the book and cover. Patrick Bock, Sara Nelson and Sean Brandt created the maps, which were adapted from the author's extensive base maps, under the supervision of U.S. Cartogrtaphy Manager Alex Guilbert. Hayden Foell drew the sidebar illustration. Lindsay Brown reviewed the Marine Life section for scientific accuracy. Portions of this text were adapted from Lonely Planet's *Eastern Caribbean*.

Lonely Planet Pisces Books

Lonely Planet acquired the Pisces line of diving and snorkeling books in 1997. The series is being developed and substantially revamped over the next few years. We welcome your comments and suggestions.

Pisces Pre-Dive Safety Guidelines

Before embarking on a scuba diving, skin diving or snorkeling trip, carefully consider the following to help ensure a safe and enjoyable experience:

- Possess a current diving certification card from a recognized scuba diving instructional agency (if scuba diving)
- Be sure you are healthy and feel comfortable diving
- Obtain reliable information about physical and environmental conditions at the dive site (e.g., from a reputable local dive operation)
- Be aware of local laws, regulations and etiquette about marine life and environment
- Dive at sites within your experience level; if possible, engage the services of a competent, professionally trained dive instructor or divemaster

Underwater conditions vary significantly from one region, or even site, to another. Seasonal changes can significantly alter site and dive conditions. These differences influence the way divers dress for a dive and what diving techniques they use.

There are special requirements for diving in any area, regardless of location. Before your dive, ask about environmental characteristics that can affect your diving and how trained local divers deal with these considerations.

Warning & Request

Things change—dive site conditions, regulations, topside information. Nothing stays the same for long. Your feedback on this book will be used to help update and improve the next edition. Excerpts from your correspondence may appear in *Planet Talk*, our quarterly newsletter, or *Comet*, our monthly email newsletter. Please let us know if you do not want your letter published or your name acknowledged.

Correspondence can be addressed to:
Lonely Planet Publications
Pisces Books
150 Linden Street
Oakland, CA 94607
email: pisces@lonelyplanet.com

Introduction

At the southernmost extreme of the Caribbean, just off the coast of Venezuela, lies the two-island republic of Trinidad and Tobago. Although the islands are linked geographically, politically and culturally, they offer very different attractions for the visitor.

LAWSON WOOD

Trinidad is the economic and political mainstay of the country. *Trinis*, as you will hear Trinidadans called, are a particularly diverse group, with large populations of islanders descended from African slaves, as well as later groups of immigrant workers from India, China and Madeira.

Only lightly touristed, Trinidad's main attraction is its impressive wildlife reserves. Virtually half of the island is still heavily forested, while other areas are occupied by savannas and mangrove swamps. It is in these undeveloped areas that you will find some 2,300 different species of flowering shrubs, including 700 types of orchids. The island hosts 57 species of bats, 70 reptile species and 108 different mammals, including a small, protected population of manatees near the southeast's Oritoire River. Most impressive is the bird population, considered the most diverse in the Caribbean—more than 400 species of birds and 620 species

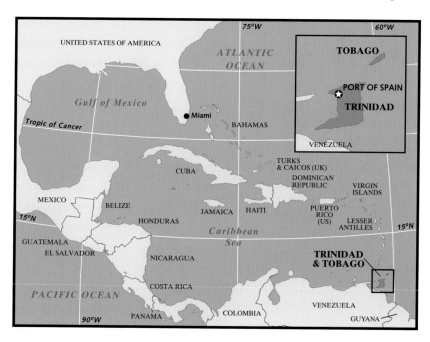

of butterflies make Trinidad their permanent home or pass through as part of their seasonal migrations.

Though most visitors come to Trinidad to enjoy bird-watching in one of several wildlife preserves, many also come to enjoy the island's annual Carnival celebration. The culmination of months of elaborate preparations, this wild and colorful street parade takes place in February or early March, during the traditional Mardi Gras (Fat Tuesday) period before Ash Wednesday. Carnival is perhaps the best time to experience Trinidad's endemic musical traditions, as several important calypso and steel pan band competitions are an integral part of the festivities.

Most visiting divers will merely pass through Trinidad en route to Tobago, the smaller and more sparsely populated "little sister" island. Though Tobago is the nation's tourism center, it has not been spoiled by development and offers beautiful beaches and world-class diving in a relaxed, unpretentious environment. Tobago's central forest reserve, the oldest protected rainforest area in the world, hosts impressive hiking and bird-watching opportunities.

Tobago's underwater opportunities range from sheltered shallow reefs appropriate for both divers and snorkelers, to challenging drift dives that will thrill the most experienced diver. Nutrients carried by the rushing Guyana Current form the basis for an impressive diversity of marine life, including some of the world's largest recorded brain corals. The island's exposure to the Atlantic Ocean also makes it an excellent place to spot pelagics, including one of the world's largest permanent populations of manta rays.

The 49 dive sites covered in this book represent a range of the best and most popular sites on both islands, divided according to island and, in Tobago, grouped into distinct diving regions. The book focuses largely on Tobago's substantial diving possibilities, but also includes sites in northwest Trinidad for the curious and adventurous diver. Information about location, depth range, access and expertise rating is provided for each site. You'll also find detailed descriptions of each site, noting conditions, underwater topography and the marine life you can expect to see. The Marine Life section provides a gallery of Trinidad and Tobago's common fish and invertebrate life. Though this book is not intended to be a standalone travel guide, the Practicalities and Overview sections offer useful information about the islands, while the Activities & Attractions section provides ideas about how to spend your time above the water.

MICHAEL LAWRENCE
Speyside is Tobago's most important diving region.

Overview

The southernmost of the Caribbean islands, Trinidad and Tobago lie southeast of Grenada, just 11km (7 miles) from South America's Venezuelan coast. Though very Caribbean in culture, the islands are geologically distinct from the Lesser Antilles, the chain of islands that separates the Caribbean Sea from the Atlantic Ocean.

MICHAEL LAWRENCE

At 4,228 square km (1,649 square miles), Trinidad is the larger of the islands and the nation's economic and governmental center. The sprawling capital, Port of Spain, is in Trinidad's northwest region. Tobago lies 33km (21 miles) northeast of Trinidad, across a shallow waterway swept by incredibly fast-moving currents. Tobago is the smaller "little sister" island, with an area of just 187 square km (73 square miles). The island's main administrative town is Scarborough, which lies on the island's more-exposed southern Atlantic shore. Visiting divers will more likely spend time in Crown Point, a resort area on the island's west end, and in the small village of Speyside, which is on the island's east end, near some of the country's premier dive sites.

History

Trinidad was the first Caribbean island settled by Amerindians who traveled to the islands from present-day Venezuela. These first inhabitants—initially Arawaks and later Caribs—populated the islands around 300 BC and gradually spread north through Tobago and the eastern Caribbean chain. Islanders hunted and fished, wove cloth and made pottery, and cultivated beans, tobacco, cassava and peppers. They traded with other Amerindian groups throughout the Caribbean. Early Spanish accounts of the Caribs—from whom the region gets its name—portray an aggressive and warlike people. Rumors of cannibalism, propagated by colonial Spaniards, are today considered unfounded.

In 1498, during his third voyage to the New World, Christopher Columbus was the first European to visit the islands. He named the island Trinidad, probably a reference to the island's three prominent mountain peaks, though the allusion to the Holy Trinity was not likely accidental. Trinidad's first colonial city was founded in 1592, but the island remained a Spanish backwater until it was taken over by the British in 1796.

Columbus sighted but never visited Tobago. Throughout the colonial period, the small island was claimed by many different colonial powers, including the British, the French, the Dutch, the Spanish and even, for a brief period, Latvian.

The nearly uninhabited island became a convenient base for pirates to raid colonial trading ships. The British finally took firm control of the island in 1815. In 1889, the British made Tobago, which previously had its own independent legislature, a ward of neighboring Trinidad.

In an effort to populate the islands, colonial powers offered land and tax concessions to emigrant settlers—largely French—from other Caribbean islands. During the 18th century, both islands developed significant plantation societies, with cultivation of tobacco, cotton, indigo and sugarcane (for rum). Plantations were tended by the slave labor of Africans brought to the islands as part of the Caribbean's massive slave trade. With a ratio of nearly 20 Africans to one white, Trinidad was home to the largest slave population in the Caribbean.

Slavery was abandoned on the islands in 1834, spelling the end of the plantation society. With the workforce at a new low, landowners encouraged immigration from other parts of the Caribbean and around the world. The most notable influx of immigrant workers came from India. By 1917, some 150,000 immigrants had arrived from India, escaping famine and a desperate economy. Today, islanders of Indian descent are commonly referred to as East Indians, a term distinguishing them from the regional West Indian moniker.

Trinidad and Tobago became an independent nation within the British Commonwealth in 1962. An oil boom in the late-1970s brought prosperity, and Trinidad and Tobago became one of the richest independent nations in the Caribbean. Heavy industry remains the backbone of Trinidad's economy, while Tobago has gained success as an international tourist destination.

Geography

Trinidad and Tobago differ from other Caribbean islands in that they are geologically related to South America. Trinidad was once part of present-day Venezuela, and the mountains on both islands are a continuation of the volcanic Andes range that traverses South America. Over 11,000 years ago, the floodwaters of Venezuela's massive Orinoco River eroded away the land, creating a channel and a jagged coastal area of northwestern Trinidad known as the Dragon's Teeth. This part of northwestern Trinidad extends toward Venezuela in a small series of islands called the Bocas Islands. The channel separating southern Trinidad from the South American coast is called the Serpent's Mouth. The Gulf of Paria, the flooded basin between Trinidad's west coast and Venezuela's Península de Paria, harbors massive fossil fuel reserves. As a result, much of the islands' economy hinges on oil and gas exports.

Trinidad's landscape consists largely of expanses of flatlands, split by three mountain ranges. The most prominent of these ranges is Northern Range, which spreads east to west and forms a backdrop for the bustling Port of Spain. The highest point on the island is found in this range above the town of Arima, the 941m (3,085ft) Cerro del Aripo.

North West Huevos Island is part of the Bocas Islands, a jagged chain extending from northwest Trinidad toward the Venezuelan coast.

The rest of the Trinidadan landscape consists of flat plains and mangrove swamps, including the Caroni Swamp and Bird Sanctuary. One peculiar feature of the Trinidadan landscape is Pitch Lake, a basin of natural asphalt formed by oil seeping into a mud volcano. Near La Brea in the southwest region, this is the largest of only three pitch lakes in the world. (The others are Rancho La Brea in Los Angeles and Guanaco in Venezuela.)

Across the shallow Columbus Passage from Trinidad, Tobago is a narrow island that stretches from the southwest to the northeast. Lowlands predominate in the west, giving way to a central mountain range that rises to 549m (1,860ft). The mountain range supports a lush rainforest habitat, the oldest protected rainforest area in the world.

Trinidad and Tobago's unique location between South America and the rest of the Caribbean makes both islands spectacular wildlife habitats. Trinidad, in particular, is a bird paradise—the island hosts some 400 different bird species, a diversity unmatched throughout the West Indies. The underwater marine environment is similarly affected by the islands' location. Divers will see tropical species native to the warmer waters of the Caribbean Sea as well as pelagic species from the colder Atlantic waters.

The seabed surrounding both islands is shallow and the average depth of the Columbus Passage is just 18m (60ft). The Guyana Current whips past rocky ridges, creating spectacular drift-diving areas, particularly on Tobago's west and east ends. The nutrient-rich Orinoco floodwaters sweep past the islands, lowering visibility in some areas, but nourishing abundant marine communities around both islands.

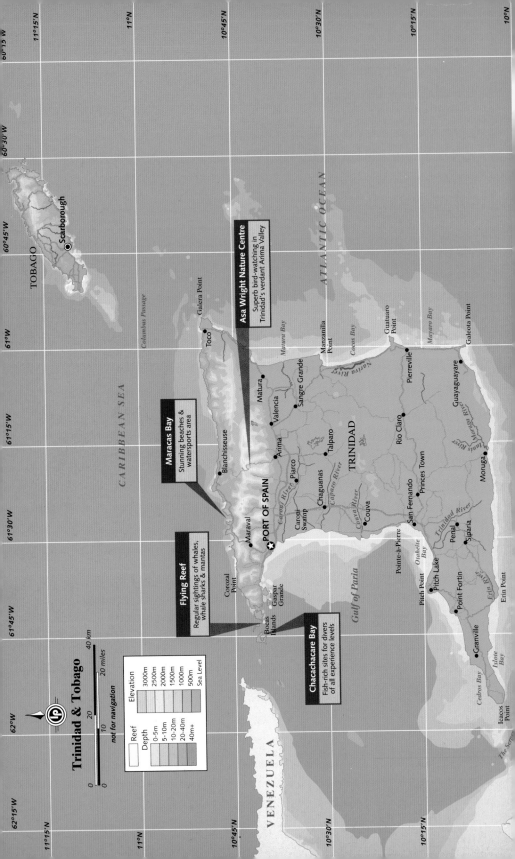

Trinidad & Tobago

Elevation

- 3000m
- 2500m
- 2000m
- 1500m
- 1000m
- 500m
- Sea Level

Depth

- Reef
- 0-5m
- 5-10m
- 10-20m
- 20-40m
- 40m+

not for navigation

0   10   20   40 km
0   20   40 miles

CARIBBEAN SEA

VENEZUELA

Chacachacare Bay
Fish-rich sites for divers of all experience levels

Flying Reef
Regular sightings of whales, whale sharks & mantas

Maracas Bay
Stunning beaches & watersports area

Asa Wright Nature Centre
Superb bird-watching in Trinidad's verdant Arima Valley

TOBAGO

Scarborough

Columbus Passage

Galera Point

Toco

Matura

Blanchisseuse

Maraval

PORT OF SPAIN

Corozal Point

Bocas Islands

Gaspar Grande

Maracas Bay

Valencia

Arima

Piarco

Chaguanas

Caroni Swamp

Sangre Grande

Talparo

TRINIDAD

Matura Bay

Manzanilla Point

Cocos Bay

Guatuaro Point

Mayaro Bay

Galeota Point

Pierreville

Rio Claro

Guayaguayare

Princes Town

Moruga

San Fernando

Couva

Pointe-à-Pierre

Otaheite Bay

Pitch Lake

Pitch Point

Point Fortin

Penal

Siparia

Erin Point

Granville

Cedros Bay

Islote Bay

Icacos Point

ATLANTIC OCEAN

Gulf of Paria

Caroni River

Cupato River

Couva River

Trinidad River

Ortoire River

Oropuche River

Moruga River

Nariva River

The Serpent

Guayaguare

CARIBBEAN SEA

Tobago

Kelleston Drain
Among the world's best sites to swim with manta rays

London Bridge
Spectacular scenic diving around a massive natural arch

Tobago Forest Reserve
Hike & bird-watch in the world's oldest protected rainforest area

Fort King George
Historic museum & arts center with beautiful coastal views

Diver's Dream
Shallow reef area swept by thrilling currents; only for experienced divers

Maverick
Challenging wreck site hosting large fish and lush invertebrate life

Mount Irvine Bay
Leatherback & green turtles come ashore to nest during spring

Buccoo Channel
Shallow reef area perfect for training dives & fish photography

Labels

Little Tobago Island
St Giles Islands
Charlotteville
Goat Island
Speyside
King's Bay
Queen's Island
North Point
Man O' War Bay
Delaford
Roxborough
Richmond Island
Cardigan Bay
L'Anse Fourmi
Bloody Bay
Sisters Rocks
Parlatuvier
Glamorgan
Goldsborough Bay
Hillsborough Dam
Smith's Island
Mount St George
Granby Point
Barbados Bay
Castara
Minister Point
Casuarua Bay
Moriah
Mason Hall
Bacolet Point
Scarborough
Rockley Bay
Fromager Bay
Plymouth
Lowlands Point
Great Courtland Bay
Stone Haven Bay
Buccoo
Bon Accord
Canoe Bay
Mount Irvine Bay
Buccoo Bay
Buccoo Reef
Crown Point International Airport
Pigeon Point
Crown Point
Milford Bay

CARIBBEAN SEA

ATLANTIC OCEAN

Reef

Depth
0-5m
5-10m
10-20m
20-40m
40m+

Elevation
1750m
1500m
1250m
1000m
500m
250m
Sea Level

4 km
3 miles
2
1.5
0

Practicalities

WOLF WINTER

Climate

Trinidad and Tobago experience a warm tropical climate tempered by seasonal offshore winds. Generally, the islands' weather patterns tend to be more closely allied to those of South America than they are to the rest of the Caribbean. The islands get about 260 mm (10 inches) of rainfall per year, mostly between June and August. The rainy season lasts from late May to mid-November, with the highest temperatures and humidity levels occurring from July to early September. Summer temperatures hover around 32°C (89°F), while the humidity level can rise to as much as 83% in August and September, particularly after a short burst of rainfall. February through May are the driest months, but short, violent rainstorms still occur and the islands are often overcast and humid. The mean dry season temperature is 29°C (84°F). Trinidad and Tobago lie well below the Caribbean's main hurricane belt and have been hit by large tropical storms in the past only rarely.

Water temperatures are highest from July to October, when they may reach 27°C (81°F). Winter water temperature drop to 18-21°C (68-71°F), with the coldest months being February and March. At many dive sites you will notice a significant thermocline below 15m (50ft).

Ol' Talk: Island Slang

English is the official language of the islands. You may also hear Hindi, Spanish and ethnic African dialects spoken. The traditional French patois has nearly died out, but everyday local speech is richly idiomatic. The following is a glossary of common slang:

bachanal	rowdy, outrageous behavior; good party
biddim **or** bim	three-quarter-length trousers
boderation	annoyance
crapaud smake yuh pipe	you are in big trouble
free up	relax, let go, shed your inhibitions
freshwater yankee	a native who returns from abroad with foreign mannerisms
jump up	a spontaneous local dance
lime	to spend time talking, laughing and flirting with passersby
play mas	put on a costume and be part of a Carnival band
ol' talk	empty chatter
sock eye	too easy for words
wine	sexy dance style where hips rotate

Getting There

American Airlines offers daily flights to Trinidad's Piarco International Airport (near Port of Spain) via Miami and New York, and weekly flights to Crown Point International Airport in Tobago via Puerto Rico. Caledonian Airways and British Airways operate two flights each week from London's Gatwick Airport directly to Tobago, while BWIA flies daily from London and Toronto to Trinidad. Condor flies to Trinidad from Frankfurt. There are daily flights from other Caribbean and South American cities on a variety of airlines, including LIAT, WINAIR and ALM. Air Caribbean regularly makes the 15-minute flight

1 Prime Minister's Residence
2 President's House
3 Rock Gardens
4 Stollmeyer's Castle
5 White Hall
6 Archbishop's Residence
7 Hayes Court
8 St Clair Medical Centre
9 National Museum & Art Gallery
10 Port of Spain General Hospital
11 Tourist Office
12 City Hall
13 Red House (Parliament)
14 Police Station
15 General Post Office
16 Cruise Ship Complex
17 Global Steamship Agencies
18 Ferries to Tobago
19 South Quay Bus Terminal
20 City Gate
21 Central Market

Port of Spain

Gulf of Paria

between Trinidad and Tobago, and offers service from the Netherlands Antilles and Caracas, Venezuela.

Several times a week, a ferry makes the five-hour journey between Trinidad and Tobago. Alternately, most of the commercial trading ships that travel between the islands take on passengers. Cruise ships dock regularly in Trinidad's Port of Spain.

Gateway Cities

Port of Spain

In Trinidad's northwest lies Port of Spain, the country's capital and commercial hub. With a population of more than 300,000, Port of Spain is a bustling urban sprawl. It is not considered a tourist city and its few high-quality hotels cater mainly to business travelers. The city center includes some impressive historic buildings from the colonial period and numerous lively pedestrian arcades to explore. Although the city is not unfriendly to tourists, it's best to avoid downtown at night unless accompanied by a local. The Piarco International Airport is a 30-minute drive southwest of the city along a wide, four-lane freeway. Expect panhandlers and street vendors to approach your car at each intersection.

Crown Point

Though not Tobago's principal commercial center (that would be Scarborough), Crown Point is the island's main tourist area and the site of the Crown Point Airport. In southwest Tobago, Crown Point hosts the island's main hotels, beaches, bars and restaurants. The airport is just a few minutes' walk from the resort areas.

Getting Around

Most visitors rent a car or travel by taxi. Look for rental car agencies in Port of Spain and Crown Point, or enlist the help of your hotel staff to arrange a car rental for you. Driving is the same as in the UK, on the left side of the road, but some of the rental cars

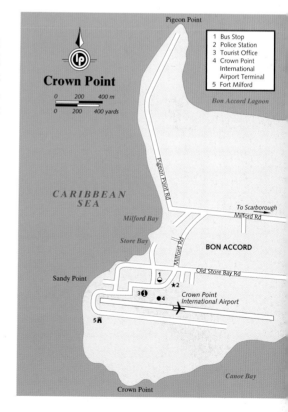

are American imports with left-hand drive, which can be confusing for visitors. The mountain ridge roads are narrow and winding, with a steep drop on one side, so take extra care. Thankfully, the interior roads tend to be quiet, so you'll be able to stop to admire the view. Tobago is more rural than Trinidad, and you should beware of stray sheep, goats and chickens—no one appears to own these wanderers until you have an accident.

Taxis are another popular way to get around the islands. They are unmetered so you'll have to negotiate prices in advance, depending on the number of passengers and the distance to be covered. Taxi service is available at the airports, though your hotel may arrange for pick-up.

Buses are a less convenient but very cheap alternative for getting around both islands. On Trinidad, express buses run between the bus stations of larger

cities. Trinidad's main station is the South Quay Bus Terminal (☎ 623-7872) in southeast Port of Spain. On Tobago, bus service is more limited. Main routes are between Crown Point and Scarborough, and Scarborough and Plymouth.

Entry

Visitors from the U.S., EEC countries and Commonwealth countries (with some exceptions, including Australia and New Zealand) do not need visas to enter Trinidad and Tobago. With a handful of exceptions, most other visitors will need visas in advance, which they must secure from the nearest consulate. Check the tourist board's website (see the Listings section) for a list of visa requirements and international consulates.

Money

The currency unit is the Trinidad and Tobago dollar (TT$), which is divided into 100 cents. You can use U.S. dollars in most places, but you should expect to receive change in TT$. Most international currencies can be exchanged at larger hotels or at local banks. Major credit cards are readily accepted at most establishments. Hotel and restaurant bills will include a 15% service charge. As always, any extra tipping is at your discretion. Taxi drivers will expect a tip if they help with luggage or are otherwise particularly helpful. Divemasters may expect a tip at the end of your dive trip, but this amount is entirely discretionary.

Time

Trinidad and Tobago are one hour ahead of Eastern Standard Time and four hours behind GMT. When it's noon in Trinidad and Tobago, it is 4pm in London, 8am in San Francisco and 1am the following morning in Sydney. Daylight saving time is not observed.

Electricity

Electrical current is both 110 and 220 volts at 60 cycles. Plugs are either American-style two-pin or British square three-pin. Twin-point shaver-style adapters are available in the bathrooms of major hotels. If you need specific voltages for recharging lamps or strobes, it's best to bring an adapter or contact the diving operation that you are using to see if they can help.

Weights & Measures

Trinidad and Tobago recently converted to the metric system—temperature is measured in degrees Celsius, length in meters and weight in grams, though you may still see and hear references to imperial measurements. Highway signs are now all in kilometers but, to add to the confusion, smaller local road signs are still in miles and locals always refer to miles when giving directions. This book provides both metric and imperial measurements, except for specific references within dive site descriptions, which are given in metric units only. For reference, use the conversion chart inside the back cover of this book.

What to Bring

Women can wear light cotton dresses, slacks and shorts at any time of the year. Topless sunbathing is not allowed on any of the beaches. For men, lightweight slacks or shorts and open-necked shirts are perfect for most occasions, while a shirt and slacks are appropriate for a fine evening. Formal dress is seldom worn, but may be required at a few of the more upscale hotels and restaurants. Swimwear is not appropriate in the main towns or in restaurants, shops, banks and post offices. It is advisable to pack a windbreaker or light raincoat and perhaps jeans and a sweatshirt as blustery squalls sometimes hit the islands. Those planning to hike the trails around the Asa Wright Nature Centre and to the various waterfalls on both islands should bring suitable waterproof gear and strong footwear.

The summer's warm water temperatures mean that a 3-4mm wetsuit will keep you sufficiently warm while affording protection against stinging marine life and the fierce sun. In the winter, water temperatures tend to be cooler than in other parts of the Caribbean, so you'll probably want to wear a full wetsuit, semi-drysuit or drysuit.

Underwater Photography

Both Trinidad and Tobago have a number of film processing locations, most of which are of the instant print variety. Trinidad has four processors that can handle E6 slide film processing on site (see the Listings section). There is no E6 film processing available on Tobago.

Business Hours

Banks are open Monday to Thursday 8am to 2pm Friday and 8am to noon and 3pm to 5pm. Other business hours are generally weekdays 8am to noon and 1pm to 4:30pm. Most shops are open weekdays 8am to 5pm and Saturday 8am to noon.

Accommodations

Much of the accommodation in both Trinidad and Tobago meets the highest modern international standards with air conditioning, private bathrooms, swimming pools and sports facilities. Some of the larger hotels and resorts have their own golf courses, most of which are world-class. Also available are much smaller and more quaint guest houses, sometimes situated in former plantation houses

The Beginner's Guide to Underwater Photography

1. Consider your photography goals and buy the best system suitable for your anticipated needs.

2. Concentrate on mastering one technique at a time. Don't try to learn everything at once.

3. Record the technical details of your photos as you take them (an underwater slate is good for this) to see which settings get the best results.

4. When using fixed focus, pre-aim your flash out of the water whenever possible.

5. To avoid backscatter in wide-angle photography, position the flash away from the camera body and at a 45° angle between the camera and subject. Never use the flash when the camera-to-subject distance is greater than one-fifth the underwater visibility.

6. Get as close as you can to your subject. Close-ups have the most impact and better color saturation. A housed 35mm camera is best for macrophotography, because you won't need to get too close to the reef.

7. To avoid shadows in close-up photography, bring the flash close to the subject and directly over the camera. Alternately, use a pair of flashes, mounted on either side of the camera.

8. Never shoot downward. Always shoot horizontally or aim upward toward your subject.

9. Note the position of the sun when you enter the water. Use the sun to create back-lit shots to add depth and interest.

10. Be ruthless. The only way to really improve is by self criticism; put as much film through the camera as possible and learn from your mistakes.

11. Attend an underwater photography course.

MICHAEL LAWRENCE

Tobago offers ample opportunities to "shoot" mantas.

and reminiscent of early colonial days. These are notable for peace, privacy and superb cuisine.

In Trinidad, hotels around Port of Spain's Queen's Park Savannah are generally the most popular. These are convenient to the Oval Cricket Ground, where each evening you can idly watch local teams playing their national sport.

In Tobago, accommodations can be found all around the island, but are concentrated mainly in Speyside and Crown Point. Most resort hotels and guest houses are affiliated with a local dive operator.

Dining & Food

Food styles in Trinidad and Tobago range from traditional Caribbean and East Indian fare to the fine international cuisine found in the larger hotels. Though many visitors tend to eat mostly in their hotels or guest houses, you should take the opportunity to sample the unique and inexpensive local delights. All over both islands you'll find small convenience stores that serve inexpensive local dishes in a casual environment and, although islanders have embraced the fast-food chains, there are still plenty of quaint, traditional eating houses. If you're looking for a quiet or romantic dining experience, try the open-air restaurants along the beach at Speyside or Charlotteville (in Tobago) or along Trinidad's north coast. Hotel restaurants and other finer restaurants will charge you tax and a 15% service charge; small local restaurants will not charge you extra, but the proprietors will expect a tip nonetheless.

Local Delicacies

The following are common local dishes served in casual restaurants and convenience stores:

black cake: a rich cake made with dried fruit, cherries, brandy and rum, iced and decorated as the traditional wedding cake

buljol: shredded flatfish with onion, tomato, avocado, pepper and olive oil

callaloo: savory green soup made with local vegetables, often flavored with hot pepper and whole blue-backed crab

doubles: curried channa (chick peas) between two bara (soft circles of fried dough) sold on the street

hops: filled crisp bread roll, as in ham 'n' hops

kibbies: a mixture of meat and corn wrapped in pastry and deep-fried

pastelles: minced-meat patties folded in corn dough, wrapped in banana leaves and steamed

pelau: peas and rice cooked with meat and flavored with coconut and pepper

phulouri: fritters made with split peas

roti: pliable folds of Indian bread cooked on a hot griddle and stuffed with curried meat or vegetables

souse: boiled pork served cold in a salty sauce with lime, cucumber, pepper and onion

Sample sugarcane and local fruit at roadside stands throughout both islands.

Shopping

Local shopping malls sell all the designer labels you might want, but look to any number of small businesses for handicrafts and locally made food products, especially sweets made with seeds, nuts, honey and coconut. Handicraft specialties include wood carvings and hats, baskets and bags woven from palm leaves and sugarcane straw. A number of shops sell woven sandals, handbags and other locally made leather goods, while other shops sell some excellent batik fabrics. Also look for exquisite silver filigree jewelry. Steel pan drums are made locally, but are very expensive—musically minded visitors can buy tapes and CDs of local steel pan, calypso and soca groups.

A Rastafarian woodcarver displays his craft.

Sounds of the Islands

In Trinidad and Tobago, the historical importance of music as social, cultural and political expression cannot be overestimated. Visitors will hear a variety of local music at any time of year, but it is at the numerous festivals and holidays throughout the year—and particularly at Carnival—that local music is highlighted.

Calypso is Trinidad and Tobago's most significant contribution to the world music scene. Also known as *kaiso*, the musical form originated in Trinidad in the late 19th century from drum and choral traditions brought to the islands by African slaves. Early calypso was sung in French, but it was the later English-speaking singers who developed highly personalized styles into competitive performances for the Carnival celebrations. Calypso first gained international notice in the 1930s, though politically charged lyrics were censored by the British Crown. Famous calypsonians like Lord Kitchener and Sparrow continued to entertain local and international audiences into the '50s and '60s.

The signature themes of calypso music are improvisation and the often-controversial expression of current happenings and sentiments. Today, the musical accompaniment is much more complex with a heavy brass section, guitars, keyboards, synthesizers and percussion. Calypso bands incorporate elaborate choreography and are considered a major part of the annual Carnival and a celebration of the islands' cultural legacy.

JIM STEPHENS FOR TIDCO
A Carnival *mas band* hits the street.

Continual experimentation and innovation have extended the calypso tradition. **Soca** (from soul-calypso) is dance-oriented party music, developing from the soul and disco music of the 1970s. Developed by the islands' East Indian communities (and frowned upon by religious leaders), **chutney soca** combines up-tempo soca rhythms with traditional Indian instruments and Hindi lyrics. **Raggo-soca** is a fusion of soca and Jamaican reggae, while **rapso** is a type of street poetry concentrating on political and social commentary.

Steel pan music is another of the more widely visible of the islands' musical traditions. Like calypso, the steel pan was born of African traditions, including the **tamboo bamboo** bands first developed by slaves as a substitute rhythm instrument for the traditional African drum. Early steel pans were merely baking pans and other basic instruments, but the art of forging oil drums into sophisticated instruments quickly developed. More than any other local musical tradition, the steel pan bands carried with them a legacy of aggression and violence, and rival steel bands often met in a form of gang warfare. It wasn't until the early 1960s that the last of the violence ceased and the Trinidad and Tobago Steel Band Association was formed. Today, top bands such as the Silver Stars are recognized worldwide. Offshoots of the steel pan music include **pan jazz**, a vibrant and soulful fusion of pan playing and jazz, and **pantar**, the imaginative blend of the sitar and the modern steel pan.

Add to this further variations—**parang** and **creche** (Christmas songs from the Spanish and French traditions), classical and contemporary East Indian music, among others—and you have an idea of the sonic landscape of Trinidad & Tobago.

Activities & Attractions

LAWSON WOOD

Tobago

Much of Tobago's tourist activity is centered along the south and southwest shore, near the wide fertile plain that stretches east from Plymouth to Scarborough. A two-hour drive along the northwest coastal road, though steep and winding in places, offers stunning vistas of Tobago's many bays. You can explore long stretches of golden sand and watch local fishermen tend their nets in the sleepy north-coast fishing communities of Castara and Parlatuvier. Other activities on the island center around its many natural wonders, including a lush rainforest habitat and opportunities for bird- and turtle-watching.

Tobago Forest Reserve

First designated for protection in 1776, the Tobago Forest Reserve is the oldest protected rainforest area in the wold. The rainforest, which lies along the island's eastern mountain ridge, was first protected to save it from indiscriminate land clearing for sugarcane cultivation. The half-hour drive between Roxborough (on the south coast) and Parlatuvier (on the north coast) brings you through the heart of the jungle and offers excellent views. Though many areas of this rocky ridge are rugged and difficult to access, there are a number of trailheads along the main road. For any serious exploration, it is wise to hire a guide—try David Rooks Nature Tours (☎ 639-4276).

The reserve is a haven to wildlife. There are 123 butterfly species (including the spectacular blue emperor butterfly), 16 lizard species, 24 snake species (non-poisonous) and 17 bat species (including one that fishes the sea at night). Also making their home in the reserve are armadillos, forest deer and even speckled caimans (a type of crocodile), which can sometimes be found lazing in the sun at Hillsborough Dam. The reserve's main attraction, however, is certainly the bird life. Some 210 bird species can be sighted

MICHAEL LAWRENCE

A rufous-tailed jacamar dines on an insect.

27

MICHAEL LAWRENCE

Set in the Tobago's lush interior, Argyll Falls offers bathers respite from the tropical heat.

here, including flycatchers, parrots, mot mots, mockingbirds and hummingbirds, while several South American species, such as black skimmers and plumbeous kites, pass through on their seasonal migration. Several local hotels along the edges of the reserve have been feeding the birds regularly for years. The evening feeding at the Arnos Vale Hotel is spectacular to watch. Similar feedings happen at the Bon Accord Lagoon next to Pigeon Point and at the Grafton Wildlife Sanctuary between Mount Irvine and Black Rock.

Argyll Falls

A 20-minute hike on an easy trail leads along a small stream and past enormous stands of bamboo and coconut palms to Argyll Falls. Offering bathers a respite from the heat and humidity, the waterfall tumbles over a series of small rocky escarpments into a deep pool at its base. Framed in exotic palms and creepers, the view is lovely. A short drive west of Roxborough, Argyll Falls can also be accessed via the cross-island road that runs through the Forest Reserve. Look for the ruins of a former plantation house near the entrance to the site. Near the entrance, you can also hire a guide who will identify flora and fauna along the trail.

Little Tobago Island

This small island east of Speyside is sometimes referred to as Bird of Paradise Island because it was once the only place in the western hemisphere to find birds of paradise in the wild. In 1909, a sanctuary was established on the island to protect a flock of 50 birds of paradise that had been imported from the Aru Islands off New Guinea. The flock thrived until 1963, when Hurricane Flora devastated the island, decimating the bird of paradise population. It is not known how many survived. Today, Little Tobago Island remains an important bird and wildlife station, hosting frigate birds, brown boobies, noddies and other tropical birds that nest all over the island. Listen for the distinctive, raucous cry of the rufous-vented chachalaca, Tobago's official bird. Most visitors come as part of a glass-bottom boat tour, touching onto the island only briefly. Serious bird-watchers can explore the island with a guide by contacting David Rooks Nature Tours.

Turtle Nesting

Gigantic leatherback turtles nest on beaches along Tobago's north shore. There are several nesting beaches in front of hotels at Plantation Beach Villas, the Seahorse Inn, Le Grand Courlan, Grafton Beach Resort and the Turtle Beach Hotel. Most properties will alert guests when nesting occurs in the early hours of the morning. The naturalist David Rooks gives weekly lectures on the ecology of this endangered species and the etiquette in approaching them without disturbing their nesting patterns. Nesting season lasts from March to July.

Leatherback Turtles

Leatherback turtles (*Dermochelys coriacea*) nest on some of Trinidad's northeast beaches and on Tobago's leeward beaches. The largest of all turtles, leatherbacks may weigh up to 540kg (1,200lbs) and reach 230cm (7½ft) in length. Like most sea turtles, leatherback populations are declining in numbers because of hunting and egg harvesting worldwide.

The nesting season runs roughly from March to July. Between nightfall and dawn, the female leatherback crawls up on the beach, uses her flippers to dig a hole, deposits 80 to 125 rubbery white eggs, covers the hole with sand and trudges back to the sea. After two months, the hatchlings emerge from the sand, make a mad dash for the ocean and swim away. Only a few will survive to maturity; however, the females that make it will eventually return to the same beach to lay their eggs.

As turtles are easily disturbed when nesting and may return to the sea prematurely if bothered, turtle watchers should remain at a distance of at least 15m (50ft) until the turtle begins laying her eggs, be completely silent and avoid shining lights. The turtle, eggs and nest area should not be touched.

A leatherback turtle painstakingly drags herself onto a Tobago beach to lay her eggs.

Glass-Bottom Boats

A glass-bottom boat tour is an easy way to take a look at the underwater world without getting wet. Many operators will combine the boat tour with a snorkel tour, allowing you to explore the shallow reefs in front of Goat Island near Speyside and Buccoo Reef in southwest Tobago. Both Frank's Glass-Bottom Boat Tours (☎ 660-5438) and Top Ranking Glass-Bottom Boat Tours (☎ 660-4904) have many years of experience in Tobago's waters.

Fort King George

Fort King George was built in 1779 by the British to protect Rockley Bay, the then-capital city now known as Scarborough. As the island changed hands several times, the fort was occupied by different colonial powers until England again took final possession. The fort has been renovated in some parts and houses the Tobago Museum. The old hospital building now contains a fine-arts center that shows the work of local and international artists. Perched on a hill at the end of Fort St., the entire complex offers commanding coastal views.

LAWSON WOOD

Flirtatious folk art at Fort King George.

Trinidad

Although the island is not known for its beaches, Trinidad's north coast offers some of the most beautiful scenery in the islands. The winding road that climbs north into the mountains from Port of Spain offers breathtaking vistas. A 45-minute drive leads to a viewing area at La Vache, where a local calypso musician will compose a song especially for you as you sip fresh coconut milk. The road continues down the north side of the mountain range and along a series of small bays. Maracas Bay shelters the island's best and most popular beach. Farther east, scenic Blanchisseuse Bay is home to a small, lively fishing village. From here the main road continues through the Yarra Forest Reserve, past the Guacharo Caves to the Asa Wright Nature Centre, where you can spend the day watching the most incredible display of exotic wild birds you are ever likely to witness. Other wildlife sanctuaries on Trinidad can be found at Pointe-à-Pierre, the Caroni Swamp, El Tucuche, Saldado Rock and on Saut d'Eau Island, which is a pelican breeding ground. You can find rare orchids in the Aripo Savannahs, and the Nariva Swamp is home to red howler monkeys, alligators, anaconda, four-eyed fish, manatees and many amphibians.

Botanical Gardens

Adjacent to the Emperor Valley Zoo, Trinidad's Botanical Gardens were laid out in 1820 and contain specimens from all over the world. The exhibits are excellent and well worth the visit to get a better understanding of the native ecology. Popular with locals and school field trips, it is a nice way to see the unique flora and fauna of the islands without the need of rubber boots or an experienced guide.

Asa Wright Nature Centre

This 80-hectare (197-acre) estate is nestled in the foothills at the head of the Arima Valley, halfway between the north coast town of Blanchisseuse and the inland town of Arima. The estate was a private cocoa, coffee and citrus plantation until 1947, when it was purchased by Dr. Newcombe Wright and his wife, Asa. The Wrights were avid naturalists and the property attracted the attention of bird-watchers and naturalists long before it was established as a non-profit conservation area and research center.

Today, the center is regarded as one of the top research facilities of its kind. The lodge has 24 rooms and a fine restaurant, and is booked far in advance by researchers, and bird-watching organizations and clubs from all over the world. Visitors can also come for the day, usually as part of a guided tour package, which can be organized by your hotel. The views of the valley are spectacular, but your eyes are constantly drawn to the hummingbirds, mot mots, channel-billed toucans, ferruginous pygmy owls, violaceous tityras, bull-throated woodcreepers, crested oropendolas and all the other wondrously named avian visitors to the center.

Set high in the Arima Valley, the Asa Wright Nature Centre offers spectacular bird-watching and commanding views of Trinidad's countryside.

Caroni Swamp & Bird Sanctuary

Caroni Swamp is probably the most popular of Trinidad's many wildlife sanctuaries because of its proximity to Port of Spain. This 4,800-hectare (12,000-acre) swamp hosts the largest breeding ground of scarlet ibis, Trinidad's official bird. Some 12,000 of these brilliantly colored birds roost in the swamplands each evening. The sanctuary's waterways are filled with large tarpon and chub, and are fringed by mangroves. The swamp is best visited during the dry season, from February through May.

Turtle Nesting

Leatherback turtles nest along Trinidad's north shore around Paria Bay, Grande Tacirib, Madamas Bay, Grande Riviere Bay and on the east coast at Matura Bay between Matura Point and Manzanilla Point. Permits for viewing turtles can be obtained from the Forestry Division (☎ 622-7476) on Long Circular Rd. in Port of Spain.

Fishing

Deep-sea fishing is a popular pastime on the islands and most hotels and dive shops run fishing trips to the outer reefs and deep water. The main catches here are wahoo, kingfish and barracuda. To arrange an excursion, talk to your hotel or dive operator, or try Hard Play Fishing Charters (☎ 639-7108).

Carnival

The king of all Caribbean Carnivals is unmistakably Trinidad's. Many Trinidadans pre-pare for Carnival with a near-consuming devotion. After New Year's Day, activities swing into full gear. The *mas camps* work late into the evenings creating costumes, the panyards are full of steel pan bands tuning up their rhythms and calypso music blasts through the night at pre-Carnival jams. A week before Carnival, preliminary competitions for the King and Queen contenders get underway.

The main Carnival festivities begin on Monday morning, two days before Ash Wednesday, with the pre-dawn J'Ouvert procession into the heart of the city. As the day proceeds, masquerade "bands" hit the streets, with members of each troupe wearing identical costumes. Tens of thousands of revelers parade and dance through-out the night and the event takes on the character of a massive street party. On Tuesday, the activities culminate with competitions for the Band of the Year and by midnight, Carnival is officially over.

Most of the larger Carnival events take place at Port of Spain's Queen's Park Savannah in the center of town, including the major steel pan band and calypso competitions.

Information on upcoming Carnivals is available from the **National Carnival Commission** (☎ 627-1530 or 627-5051).

JIM STEPHENS FOR TIDCO

LAWSON WOOD

Diving Health & Safety

General Health

Both Trinidad and Tobago are generally healthy destinations that pose no serious health risks to most visitors. If you are planning to travel extensively in rural areas, however, consider getting vaccinations for hepatitis A, typhoid and yellow fever. The main danger to most visitors is usually the sun—use plenty of sunscreen or cover up well to prevent sunburn, and be sure to drink plenty of water to prevent dehydration.

The U.S. Centers for Disease Control & Prevention regularly posts updates on health-related concerns around the world specifically for travelers. Contact the CDC by fax or visit their website. Call (toll-free from the U.S.) ☎ 888-232-3299 and request Document 000005 to receive a list of documents available by fax. The website is www.cdc.gov.

Pre-Trip Preparation

Your general state of health, diving skill level and specific equipment needs are the three most important factors that impact any dive trip. If you honestly assess these before you leave, you'll be well on your way to assuring a safe dive trip.

First, if you're not in shape, start exercising. Second, if you haven't dived for a while (six months is too long) and your skills are rusty, do a local dive with an experienced buddy or take a scuba review course. Finally, inspect your dive gear. Feeling good physically, diving with experience and with reliable equipment will not only increase your safety, but will also enhance your enjoyment underwater.

At least a month before your trip, inspect your dive gear. Remember, your regulator should be serviced annually, whether you've used it or not. If you use a dive computer and can replace the battery yourself, change it before the trip or buy a spare one to take along. Otherwise, send the computer to the manufacturer for a battery replacement.

If possible, find out if the dive center rents or services the type of gear you own. If not, you might want to take spare parts or even spare gear. A spare mask is always a good idea.

Purchase any additional equipment you might need, such as a dive light and tank marker light for night diving, a line reel for wreck diving, etc. Make sure you have at least a whistle attached to your BC. Better yet, add a marker tube (also known as a safety sausage or come-to-me).

Get hepatitis A, typhoid or yellow fever immunizations if you'll need them and fill prescriptions. Certain immunizations and treatments might need to begin several months before you leave.

About a week before taking off, do a final check of your gear, grease o-rings, check batteries and assemble a save-a-dive kit. This kit should at minimum contain extra mask and fin straps, snorkel keeper, mouthpiece, valve cap, zip ties and o-rings. Don't forget to pack a first-aid kit and medications such as decongestants, ear drops, antihistamines and seasickness tablets.

Diving & Flying

Most divers in Trinidad & Tobago arrive by plane. While it's fine to dive soon *after* flying, it's important to remember that your last dive should be completed at least 12 hours (some experts advise 24 hours, particularly after repetitive dives) *before* your flight to minimize the risk of decompression sickness, caused by residual nitrogen in the blood.

Tips for Evaluating a Dive Operator

First impressions mean a lot. Does the business appear organized and professionally staffed? Does it prominently display a dive affiliation such as NAUI, PADI, SSI, BSAC, etc.? These are both good indications that it adheres to high standards.

When you come to dive, a well-run business will always have paperwork for you to fill out. At the least, someone should look at your certification card and ask when you last dived. If they want to see your logbook or check basic skills in the water, even better.

Rental equipment should be well rinsed. If you see sand or salt crystals, watch out, as their presence could indicate sloppy equipment care. Before starting on your dive, inspect the equipment thoroughly: Check hoses for wear, see that mouthpieces are secure and make sure they've given you a depth gauge and air pressure gauge.

After you gear up and turn on your air, listen for air leaks. Now test your BC: Push the power inflator to make sure it functions correctly and doesn't free-flow; if it fails, get another BC—don't try to inflate it manually; make sure the BC holds air. Then purge your regulator a bit and smell the air. It should be odorless. If you detect an oily or otherwise bad smell, try a different tank, then start searching for another operator.

DAN

Divers Alert Network (DAN) is an international membership association of individuals and organizations sharing a common interest in diving and safety. It operates a 24-hour diving emergency hotline in the U.S.: ☎ 919-684-8111 or 919-684-4DAN (-4326). The latter accepts collect calls in a dive emergency. Though DAN does not directly provide medical care, it does provide advice on early treatment, evacuation and hyperbaric treatment of diving-related injuries. Divers should contact DAN for assistance as soon as a diving emergency is suspected.

DAN membership is reasonably priced and includes DAN TravelAssist, a membership benefit that covers medical air evacuation from anywhere in the world for any illness or injury. For a small additional fee, divers can get secondary insurance coverage for decompression illness. For membership questions, contact DAN at ☎ 800-446-2671 in the U.S. or ☎ 919-684-2948 elsewhere. DAN can also be reached at www.diversalertnetwork.org.

Dive boats in Tobago tend to be simple pirogue-style boats and are often uncovered.

Medical & Recompression Facilities

Trinidad's main hospital is the **Port of Spain General Hospital** (☎ 623-2951) on Charlotte St., but most foreign visitors use the **St. Clair Medical Centre** (☎ 628-1451) on Elizabeth St., also in Port of Spain. Tobago's **General Hospital** (☎ 639-2551) is in Scarborough. Though there are plenty of pharmacies on both islands, visitors should bring sufficient medication for their needs as foreign prescriptions cannot be filled. In a pinch, a pharmacist can recommend a local physician who can issue a new prescription. Trinidad and Tobago's emergency numbers are ☎ 999 for police and ☎ 990 for fire or ambulance.

Trinidad has a full hyperbaric **recompression facility** (☎ 623 2951) in Port of Spain. Thanks to the hard work of volunteers from the Tobago Dive Association, Tobago also has a **recompression chamber** (☎ 660-4000) in Roxborough.

Drift-Diving Safety

Swept by the intense Guyana Current, Tobago is known worldwide for its exciting and challenging drift dives. The essential difference between a drift dive and other open water dives is that on a drift dive, you allow the current to carry you along. Rather than mooring in one place, the dive boat follows your group, picking you up at the end of your dive.

Drift diving can be fun, but divers should be aware of the potential dangers and take extra precautionary measures. The dangers of drift diving are twofold: the main danger is of being swept away from your group, while the secondary danger is of being injured when a current sweeps you toward a rocky pinnacle or island. Tobago dive operators are well accustomed to this type of diving and do their best to ensure that you have a safe diving experience. The following tips will help to lessen your likelihood of being the subject of a search and rescue mission:

- Tobago's drift dives should only be undertaken when the conditions are calm. Rough seas lessen your chances of being seen by the dive boat should you become separated from the group.

- All divers must always carry sufficient signaling devices. You should have a marker tube, a signal light and a whistle. The best marker tubes are brightly colored and about 3m (10ft) high. They roll up and can easily fit into a BC pocket or be clipped onto a D-ring. They're inflated orally or with a regulator.

- Your divemaster will be attached to a surface marker buoy, which floats on the surface and allows the dive boat to track the group's position underwater. Always know where your divemaster is.

- Stay with the group. Resist any temptations to dive off on your own, as to do so may bring you out of sight of the dive boat and cause you to become lost.

- Know your skill level. If you are unsure of your ability to undertake any given dive, consult your divemaster.

- Don't do drift dives at night or during twilight. If you get swept away from your group, the darkness will make it much harder for the dive boat to find you.

Diving in Trinidad & Tobago

MICHAEL LAWRENCE

Of the two islands, Tobago is unquestionably the primary diving center, with more-favorable conditions and more diving operators and diveable regions than Trinidad. Low visibility and little diving infrastructure limit Trinidad's underwater appeal, but adventurous divers can encounter a surprising variety of marine life around the northwest's offshore islands.

Diving in Trinidad and Tobago is largely defined by the islands' unique location, in the flow of South America's Guyana Current and at the confluence of the Caribbean Sea and the Atlantic Ocean. The Guyana Current makes Tobago an internationally recognized area for challenging and exciting drift dives, which can range from a gentle push to an exhilaratingly wild ride. The nutrient-rich current fosters spectacular growth of the area's barrel sponges, sea fans and, most impressively, brain corals, which are among the largest recorded in the world. The nutrients in the current are also the basis for an impressive food chain that attracts larger hunting pelagics both from the Caribbean and from the colder Atlantic waters. Most notable of these pelagics are the manta rays, which are commonly seen at many of Tobago's best-known dive sites, especially in the Speyside region.

At many sites, water conditions are often rough, so not every site will be diveable on any given day. In fact, rough weather can blow you out of entire regions for days at a time. On most days, however, at least one of Tobago's dive regions will have sufficiently calm conditions. Tobago's dive operators are accustomed to rough conditions and will often query you on your readiness for especially challenging dives. If you are unsure of your ability to undertake a particular dive, seek advice from your dive operator or divemaster.

Nearly all the diving off both islands is by boat, mostly using open pirogue-style boats on Tobago and custom dive boats on Trinidad. Because most sites aren't far from shore, the dive boat will usually return to shore after each dive unless a two-tank trip has been planned in advance. No live-aboards currently operate in Trinidad and Tobago.

Certification

If you have never dived before, it is possible to learn in Trinidad and Tobago. All the diving centers offer instruction, sometimes in a variety of languages. Another option for first-timers is a resort course, which consists of a half-day classroom orientation, swimming pool practice and a tryout dive to a shallow reef. A resort course does not provide certification. Many of the dive sites, even well-known sites in the popular Speyside area, are challenging drift dives and may have poor underwater visibility. These conditions can make Trinidad and Tobago a less-than-ideal place for trainees and other novice divers.

Snorkeling

Though diving is the main marine attraction on the islands, there are a few good snorkeling opportunities for nondivers. Tobago's several shallow reefs are perfect for visitors who want to experience the underwater environment without going too far under. Popular Tobago snorkel sites are in the southwest, off Pigeon Point

Diving into History

Though Trinidad and Tobago are not regarded as major wreck-diving areas, the islands' waters have seen the destruction of hundreds of ships throughout the region's checkered history. In addition to Tobago's dive-able *Maverick* site, known wrecks include remains of Spanish galleons just inside Scarborough's harbor, former pirate ships in the Columbus Passage and dozens of World War II-era troop and supply carriers. These "mysteries of the deep" have long held a lure for treasure hunters and researchers, whose efforts have contributed greatly to our knowl-edge of the region.

A French angelfish explores Trinidad's *Baltima Quasea* (Angostura Wreck).

The waters around Trinidad in particular yield an astounding num-ber of mostly undiveable WWII wrecks, largely from a significant German military attack that took place in 1942. Targeting the area between Aruba, Curaçao and Trinidad, German U-boats and Italian submarines were responsible for the sinking of over 400 merchant ships. An estimated 7,000 Allied merchant seamen lost their lives. Virtually all the ships went down in deep water, but a number were lost on the shallow reefs between Trinidad and Tobago, some of which have been charted, recorded and salvaged by archival research divers.

Most of the underwater wreck research around the islands has been carried out by Gaylord Kelshall, the president of Trinidad's **Chaguaramas Military History and Aviation Museum** (☎ 634-4391). Museum exhibits focus on some of the wrecks, offer-ing incredible insight into those troubled times. Qualified wreck divers should contact the museum's diving club for information about participating in archival research dives.

and Buccoo Reef, where reef formations lie close to the shoreline. Speyside's Goat Island is also appropriate for snorkeling, but you'll have to dive from a boat. On the western north coast, Arnos Vale and Great Courland Bays also have good protected reefs that are accessible from the shore. Trinidad's snorkeling is less impressive, but suitable spots include sites around Chacachacare and Saut d'Eau Islands.

Dive Site Icons

The symbols at the beginning of each dive site description provide a quick summary of some of the important characteristics of each site:

 Good snorkeling or free-diving site.

 Remains or partial remains of a wreck can be seen at this site.

 Sheer wall or drop-off.

 Deep dive. Features of this dive are found in water deeper than 27m (90ft).

 Strong currents may be encountered at this site.

 Strong surge (the horizontal movement of water caused by waves) may be encountered at this site.

 Drift dive. Because of strong currents and/or difficulty in anchoring, a drift dive is recommended at this site.

 Shore dive. This site can be accessed from shore.

 Poor visibility. The site often has visibility of less than 8m (25ft).

 Caves or caverns are a prominent feature of this site. Only experienced cave divers should explore inner cave areas.

 Marine preserve. Special protective regulations apply in this area.

Pisces Rating System for Dives & Divers

The dive sites in this book are rated according to the following diver skill-level rating system. These are not absolute ratings but apply to divers at a particular time, diving at a particular place. For instance, someone unfamiliar with prevailing conditions might be considered a novice diver at one dive area, but an intermediate diver at another, more familiar location.

Novice: A novice diver should be accompanied by an instructor, divemaster or advanced diver on all dives. A novice diver generally fits the following profile:
◆ basic scuba certification from an internationally recognized certifying agency
◆ dives infrequently (less than one trip a year)
◆ logged fewer than 25 total dives
◆ little or no experience diving in similar waters and conditions
◆ dives no deeper than 60ft (18m)

Intermediate: An intermediate diver generally fits the following profile:
◆ may have participated in some form of continuing diver education
◆ logged between 25 and 100 dives
◆ dives no deeper than 130ft (40m)
◆ has been diving in similar waters and conditions within the last six months

Advanced: An advanced diver generally fits the following profile:
◆ advanced certification
◆ has been diving for more than two years and logged over 100 dives
◆ has been diving in similar waters and conditions within the last six months

Regardless of your skill level, you should be in good physical condition and know your limitations. If you are uncertain of your own level of expertise for a particular site, ask the advice of a local dive instructor. He or she is best qualified to assess your abilities based on the site's prevailing dive conditions. Ultimately, however, you must decide if you are capable of making a particular dive, a decision that should take into account your level of training, recent experience and physical condition, as well as the conditions at the site. Remember that conditions can change at any time, even during a dive.

Tobago Dive Sites

Tobago's nutrient-rich waters—fed by both the warm Gulf Stream and the colder upwelling Guyana Current—support a wide variety of marine life. This strong current can, however, reduce visibility significantly. Tobago is not regarded for crystal-clear water, but its waters support an abundance of marine life and provide some of the best drift diving in the Caribbean. Represented here are many of the fish and invertebrate species found throughout the eastern Caribbean and western Atlantic, as well as many uncommon and even rare species, such as toadfish and shortnose batfish. Look also for seaweed blenny, yellowprow goby and snook. The main lure for many divers is the likelihood—and near certainty in some locations—of diving with large pelagic fish, which are attracted by the abundant food supply of both fish and plankton. Perhaps most notably, Tobago is one of the few places in the world where you can regularly dive with manta rays.

Diving is concentrated in five main areas around the island: Speyside, the St. Giles Islands, Man O' War Bay, the North Coast and the Columbus Passage. Most dive shops are located in either Speyside (on the east coast) or Pigeon Point (on the west coast), though you will find a few operators in other places around the island, such as Charlotteville and Buccoo Bay. Most hotels have a small branch office of a local dive shop, where you can get information and arrange dive trips all over the

LAWSON WOOD

Speyside dive sites are situated at the confluence of the Caribbean Sea and the Altantic Ocean.

island. Operators use local pirogue-style open boats, which are not always sheltered from the sun. However, most dive sites are just a short ride from the port, and guides usually do only a single dive before heading back.

You can dive around Tobago at any time of the year, but you may encounter some fairly rough seas during the stormy summer months (July through September). However, since it is a small island, the lee shore is never far away. The small offshore islands, such as Little Tobago Island and the St. Giles Islands, tend to be especially susceptible to rough weather. Because of the strong year-round currents, most Tobago dives are drift dives, which range from gentle drifts that require some swimming to fast rip currents that can sweep you around submarine islands and along cliff walls at an exhilarating speed. Divers should have drift-diving experience and must be accompanied by a divemaster carrying a surface marker buoy.

Tobago has a few true coral reefs, such as Angel Reef (off Goat Island) and the massive Buccoo Reef (off the north coast). Rare corals include several species of cup coral, and red-polyp octocoral can be found in sheltered areas. Though not as diverse as in other parts of the Caribbean, the coral is in excellent health and there are some very large mature specimens. The brain coral heads—often reported as the largest in the world—are particularly notable. The most massive of these corals are hundreds of years old and span more than 4m (13ft) across. You can find thousands of barrel, rope and tube sponges on the reefs, which are home to countless invertebrates, hydroids and fish.

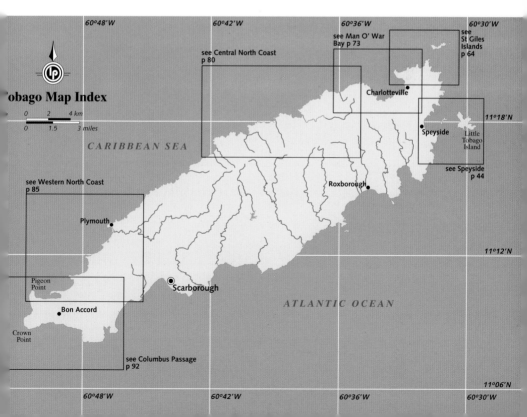

Speyside Dive Sites

The whole region along the mostly sheltered east coast is referred to as Speyside, after the small dive-oriented village on the shores of Tyrrel's Bay. The diving here is regarded as some of the best in Tobago because of abundant giant manta rays, schools of tarpon and sharks. Divers and underwater photographers come here year after year to see the famed majestic giant brain corals and the millions of tiny fish.

LAWSON WOOD

Goat Island is just five minutes from Speyside by boat.

Much of the diving is concentrated around Little Tobago Island and Goat Island, as well as their satellite rocks and offshore islands. The majority of these are drift dives and many areas are subject to surge. When conditions are calm, dive operators may extend their diving range and travel out of the bay and south along the rugged coastline or to the exposed eastern shore of Little Tobago Island.

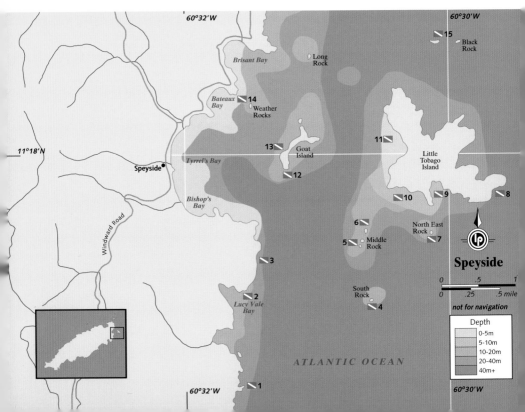

Speyside Dive Sites

	Good Snorkeling	Novice	Intermediate	Advanced
1 Inner Space				●
2 Lucifer's Bay			●	
3 Spiny Bay			●	
4 South Rock (Shark Bank)				●
5 Bookends			●	
6 Alps			●	
7 TD's Special				●
8 Picker				●
9 Black Jack Hole	●	●		
10 Kelleston Drain			●	
11 Flying Manta (Cathedral)	●	●		
12 Japanese Gardens	●	●		
13 Angel Reef	●	●		
14 Bateaux Reef (Aquamarine)	●	●		
15 Sleeper				●

1 Inner Space

A 30-minute boat ride from Speyside's port, Inner Space is dived only rarely, in part because it commonly experiences a heavy ground swell and large breakers. With so many excellent sites near the inner islands and bay, most dive operators don't consider Inner Space worth the effort. However, when you can persuade an operator to take you to this eastern wall, you will not be disappointed. This distant site generally hosts different fish species than the ones found closer to Speyside.

Location: South of Lucy Vale Bay

Depth Range: 8-30m (27-100ft)

Access: Boat

Expertise Rating: Advanced

A series of submarine peaks rises from the sandy seabed at 45m to around 22m. The pinnacles are festooned with coral and sponge growth, particularly antler, yellow tube and azure vase sponges. On the walls, gorgonians and orange sea fans extend their feeding polyps into the current. Look for large schools of chromis and wrasse around the tops of the pinnacles—these small fish are the prey of passing tarpon and various species of jack.

A French angelfish patrols a colorful Tobago reef.

2 Lucifer's Bay

It is a shame that dive boats rarely travel this far south of the safe haven of Speyside, as the site is well worth the extra effort. Coral growth in this area is sparse because of the often-surgy conditions, but there are zillions of small fish to keep you interested. The bicolor damselfish are especially striking—as they flit over the reef, their white tail tips will catch your attention. Creole wrasse and brown chromis are also commonly found here.

At Lucifer's Bay, massive boulders tumble down the steeply sloping wall to the seabed. The rocky slope drops down to 21m, where you'll find peacock flounders on the undulating sandy plain. Stingrays are also common, as are numerous other sand-loving creatures. You'll start deep, but as you proceed north, the rocky slope to your left eventually starts to flatten out and the sand slopes up toward shallower water, where you'll finish your dive. Sea urchins are common and should always be treated with caution as their sharp spines can easily penetrate skin through neoprene.

Location: South of Tyrrel's Bay

Depth Range: 15-21m (50-70ft)

Access: Boat

Expertise Rating: Intermediate

Nurse sharks are regularly seen along the wall, as are lobsters and large crabs.

Be careful of the sea urchin's long, sharp spines.

3 Spiny Bay

A jungle of trailing cactus clings to the cliffs above Spiny Bay—the cacti appear to survive quite happily in this sea-soaked environment. The cliffs extend underwater in rocky ridges and, although coral growth is sparse, the ridges are decorated with hydroids, tunicates and small sponges.

The sandy seabed at 12m is dotted with small coral heads, which are home to a wide variety of marine life. Snake eels, spotted drums, peacock flounders and goatfish are common where the

Location: South of Tyrrel's Bay

Depth Range: 3-12m (10-40ft)

Access: Boat

Expertise Rating: Intermediate

reef meets the sand. Divers should also look out into the blue, as there is a good chance of seeing large tarpon and even green or hawksbill turtles.

Dive conditions here are prone to oceanic surges and currents, which are likely to push you north toward the point where the cliffs end and Tyrrel's Bay begins. Conditions can be dangerous, particularly around the base of the cliffs. When approaching the surface, you should swim out into the open water away from the cliffs, so you can be picked up by the dive boat safely and easily.

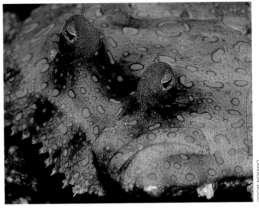

Peacock flounders inhabit the area's sandy plains.

Tunicates: Spineless Chordates

One of the Caribbean's most common marine invertebrates, tunicates are often mistaken for sponges. Like the sponge, they usually have two siphons, one for drawing in nutrients and the other for expelling used water. Though some are free-swimming, most tunicates are attached at one end and come in a variety of often-brilliant colors. Sometimes the tunicate will be covered in algal growth, making it difficult to spot unless it is feeding and its siphon is open. These creatures are difficult to photograph because they are light and pressure sensitive—when disturbed, muscular bands around the siphons rapidly contract. The common name "tunicate" comes from the animal's cellulose body covering or "tunic." They are also commonly called "sea squirts" because some species, when irritated, will forcefully expel a stream of water from their excurrent opening. Tunicates can live singularly or in a colony, and sometimes a number of compound tunicates will live together inside a common tunic with multiple incurrent siphons and a larger excurrent siphon.

Perhaps most unique about the tunicate is its seemingly unusual classification. Normally, chordates have backbones and are vertebrates. Not so with the tunicate. Classified as a urochordate, the tunicate has no backbone, but is still included in the Chordata phylum. Why? At some point in the life cycle, all urochordates have a tail, a dorsal central spinal cord, pharyngael gill clefts and, at the larval stage, a notochord, which is a flexible, supportive rod made of cartilage. In vertebrates, the notochord is replaced by bone.

4 South Rock (Shark Bank)

This isolated rock, found well east of Spiny Bay and south of Little Tobago Island, is subject to strong currents. You will spend part of the dive fighting against the current to get around the corner of the sheer-sided rock. After this, the current runs in your favor on the other side. Because of these challenging conditions, South Rock is rarely dived.

Location: South of South Rock

Depth Range: 6-30m (20-100ft)

Access: Boat

Expertise Rating: Advanced

The shallowest portion of the rock, from the wave line to around 6m, is smothered in fire coral, which merges into a bed of brightly colored sponges, large colonial hydroids and sea squirts. Gorgonian sea fans decorate the deeper vertical walls. As you might expect from the site's name, your chances of encountering nurse and blacktip sharks here are very high. It is also common to see large individual tarpon in this area, many of which grow to more than 2m long. Because of their large size and their upright triangular dorsal fins, divers often mistake tarpon for sharks.

LAWSON WOOD

The islands' most commonly seen shark is the nurse shark.

5 Bookends

The name of this dive site refers to a pair of rocks with a vertical cut between them, which makes the rocks look like bookends. When conditions are perfect, Bookends is a favorite of divers, though it can be challenging in a strong current. The conditions can be dangerous—if you descend on the wrong side of the rocks, the current can whisk you off into deep water or up over the top of the reef, where you could be tossed onto the jagged rocks. If you plan the dive correctly, you will descend and pick up a current that will

Location: Near Middle Rock

Depth Range: 7-24m (23-80ft)

Access: Boat

Expertise Rating: Intermediate

sweep you around into the more sheltered Tyrrel's Bay area, where the reef wall extends north to Little Tobago Island. A good dive guide will assess the conditions and brief you thoroughly before you take the plunge.

At around 7m you'll find a natural amphitheater carved out of the rock, where nurse sharks often rest. The reef drops steeply from the rock and coral lip to a sandy seabed at about 25m. Corals, sea fans and sea rods are interspersed with large yellow tube, brown antler and barrel sponges. The much rarer strawberry vase sponge can also be seen growing on the stalks of sea plumes.

Above the reef in the open water column swim literally thousands of creole wrasse and blue chromis. These fish are hunted by the area's permanent residents—huge tarpon—which will approach you as they patrol their domain.

One of many large tarpon at Bookends.

Tarpon Tales

Tarpon (*Megalops atlanticus*) are long silvery fish that are distinguished by their up-turned mouths. Because of their size—up to 2m (7ft) in length—and their upright dorsal fins, divers sometimes mistake them for sharks. Tarpon are renowned game fish, known for their tremendous fighting ability when hooked. Luckily for them, tarpon meat is definitely not worth tasting.

A female tarpon lays 13 million eggs in a single spawn, but very few of these eggs survive to become fully grown. During they day, you will often see tarpon in large schools, swimming slowly around reefs, sea grass areas, canals and other secluded spots. At night they hunt either alone or in pairs, working in tandem to attack small schools of fish.

—*Reef Line*, the newsletter of Reef Relief

6 Alps

A rocky cleft cuts through the wall that extends from Bookends and runs toward Little Tobago Island. Though it's hardly as impressive as the famed European mountain range, the terrain is sufficiently rocky to warrant the name "Alps."

Large barrel sponges, strawberry vase sponges and tube sponges cover the reef. Along the slope, you'll find many different coral species, including pencil coral, star coral and the much larger

Location: South of Little Tobago Island

Depth Range: 12-20m (40-66ft)

Access: Boat

Expertise Rating: Intermediate

boulder star coral. These corals tend to be surrounded by cleaning gobies, which wait patiently for passing fish to come to be cleaned of parasites and other irritants. This area is also known for the large number of queen angelfish and the millions of small fish that are found along the reef wall. Patrolling tarpon swim along the wall, as do various jacks, tangs, parrotfish and triggerfish.

A whitespotted filefish (in its unspotted orange phase) feeds among the fish fry.

7 TD's Special

Along the south shore of Little Tobago Island and south of Black Jack Hole (Dive Site #9), a lonely group of rocks breaks the surface. These rocks are home to an obvious surge that creates an area of breaking waves and white water. It is easy to see why TD's Special should only be dived when seas are calm and conditions are nearly perfect. The site tends to be most diveable around April or May, when it can be suitable for diving for weeks on end. At other times of the year, it may be diveable for a couple of days at a time. Stay deeper than the steep and often vertical rocks to avoid the worst of the surge and white water, which can be a real problem near the surface.

Location: North East Rock

Depth Range: 12-40m (40-130ft)

Access: Boat

Expertise Rating: Advanced

With these rough conditions, there is hardly any sponge growth along the circular route of this rocky massif, and even the encrusting corals are small and stunted. The rocky walls, however, are covered in hydroids, tunicates and bryozoans. Look for hermit crabs, arrow

MICHAEL LAWRENCE

Speyside is one of few places in the world where divers can regularly swim with manta rays.

crabs, small spotted lobsters, shrimp and large anemones.

The site is well named—its "specialty" is schools of fish that are not normally seen in schools, such as big-eye snapper.

The current that passes by these offshore rocky seamounts attracts large numbers of tarpon, horse-eye jacks, almaco jacks and needlefish. TD's Special should not be missed when diving in the region.

8 Picker

Along the eastern wall of Little Tobago Island, Picker is only dived in exceptional circumstances, perhaps a few times each month, when the might of the Atlantic swell dies down sufficiently to allow for safe diving. It is a favorite site of local divemasters, so if conditions warrant it, they can be persuaded to take you to this nearly vertical wall that drops below 40m. The water is generally quite clear along this exposed wall, which greatly increases the visual splendor of the dive.

Though the site is subject to extreme currents that can whip you around the exposed headland, there are a few sheltered spots behind some of the larger corals and rocky ridges. Look for lobsters and nurse sharks in these safer spots.

Location: Southeast of Little Tobago Island

Depth Range: 7-40m (23-130ft)

Access: Boat

Expertise Rating: Advanced

Schools of pelagic jacks, barracuda, tarpon and triggerfish are always seen in the area and, although the upper reaches of the cliff are bare of good corals, small encrusting sponges cover the site. As the boulder slope drops away to deep water, look for large gorgonian sea fans, rods and plumes.

9 Black Jack Hole

Off the south shore of Little Tobago Island, Black Jack Hole is considered the easier precursor to the Kelleston Drain dive—it's easier because the current is not as fast in this area and is a precursor because it ends where the Kelleston Drain begins. Though named after the frequently seen schools of black jacks, the dive is probably better known for the massive schools of creole wrasse and blue chromis that absolutely fill the water column, parting as you make your way along the reef slope.

The dive starts in a small sheltered bay surrounded by sheer rocky cliffs.

Location: South of Little Tobago Island

Depth Range: 6-21m (20-70ft)

Access: Boat

Expertise Rating: Novice

Most divers begin safely out of the current by descending to a coral rubble plain at 6m. From here the reef slopes steadily downward. The healthy growth of finger corals, pencil corals, small sea fans and sea plumes gradually gives way to larger boulder, star and brain corals interspersed with massive barrel sponges.

As you venture farther from the shore, the current picks up and begins to whisk you along the edge of the reef slope toward the next headland, where your dive boat waits to pick you up. As the current increases, so do the types and sizes of fish, coral and sponge species. The sea plumes here are like huge, draping willow trees and host fingerprint cyphomas, which are considered rare in other areas of the Caribbean. The slope levels out as you approach the small plateau found to the southeast at around 11m. The corals and sponges in this area are spaced more widely apart, and you may find flounders, small stingrays, yellowhead jawfish and gobies resting in the sandy patches.

On this dive, listen for a mysterious continuous croaking that sounds remarkably like a terrestrial toad. Curious and persistent divers will be rewarded if they track down the sound's source—the large-eye toadfish. Toadfish live in coral hollows, which they use to magnify their distinctive call. This call helps them declare their territory and advertise for a mate. Distinguished by large, wide-set eyes, a flattened body shape and fleshy barbells under the chin, the toadfish around Tobago are cousins of the species commonly seen in Cozumel and Honduras.

Black Jack Hole is often dived at night, but the current can make night diving quite frustrating. You rarely get the chance to stop and concentrate on the reef life for fear of losing your divemaster!

LAWSON WOOD
A moray eel roams the reef on its nighttime feeding.

10 Kelleston Drain

This dive starts at a coral plateau just off the southwest point of Black Jack Hole. From here, the current quickly whisks you over the plateau into deeper water, where the coral and sponge growth is much more profuse. The nutrient-rich current not only feeds the sponges and smaller corals, but also nurtures what is regarded as the single largest brain coral in the Caribbean, and possibly the largest in the world. This boulder brain coral is so distinctively massive—more than 6m across and 4m high—that it can be difficult to take in as you sweep past in the current.

At the edge of the wide, steeply sloping sandy plain, you are likely to see nurse sharks and other pelagics. Tobago has become world famous for one pelagic species in particular—the manta

Location: Southwest corner of Little Tobago Island

Depth Range: 9-15m (30-50ft)

Access: Boat

Expertise Rating: Intermediate

ray. Mantas are often referred to locally as "Tobago taxis," because they are incredibly common. In fact, mantas appear on more than 70% of the dives around Little Tobago Island. These graceful giants have become so accustomed to seeing divers that they remain completely unperturbed by your presence and will often stay with you as long as your air allows.

LAWSON WOOD

Biggest Brain in the Caribbean

The coral most associated with Tobago diving is undoubtedly the gigantic form of the boulder brain coral (*Colpophyllia natans*). In Tobago, these corals have attained record proportions, some of them more than 4m (13ft) across and one famed monstrosity more that 6m (20ft) wide. Single large specimens are found around the Kelleston Drain area off the southwest corner of Little Tobago Island, while large groups of brain corals more than 2m (7ft) across are found around the St. Giles Islands to the north of Tobago.

The grooves across the coral's surface give this species of stony coral its apt name. The ridges of the coral are normally brown or tan, while the valleys are generally green or tan. The coral's feeding polyps lie within the grooves, extending at night to feed. Small cleaning gobies lurk in the grooves as they wait to groom passing fish.

It is surmised that the corals in this area grow so large because of the almost constant tidal current, which carries nutrient-rich waters north from South America and southeast from the Caribbean. The passing planktonic particles fuel these giant communities, making them the largest known corals in the Caribbean, and among the largest brain corals in the world.

11　Flying Manta (Cathedral)

Flying Manta starts along the western shore of Little Tobago Island, in a coral rubble area at around 6m. The rubble is dotted with small scrubby sea fans that improve in stature and quality as you descend the steeply sloping fringe reef. The corals and sponges here are in good condition.

This site is named after its predominant attraction—a chance to swim

Location: West of Little Tobago Island

Depth Range: 2-20m (6-66ft)

Access: Boat

Expertise Rating: Novice

with manta rays. The southwest corner of Little Tobago Island—where some divemasters begin the dive—is known as the mantas' favored spot, but the current is often too severe. Divers are advised to keep to the shallower waters toward the end of the dive, where it is also possible to see mantas.

A natural bay allows for a safe exit from the current. The visibility drops in the shallow areas but you'll be

LAWSON WOOD

The manta's fleshy mandibles funnel plankton into its mouth.

rewarded with large numbers of tropical fish, including angelfish, butterflyfish, parrotfish, wrasse, blennies and gobies. Boulder and star corals are widely spaced, while elkhorn corals shelter snappers and grunts under their branches.

You should finish the dive before you reach the northwest corner of Little Tobago Island as the difficult tidal and current conditions beyond could sweep you off. The dive boat will have difficulty finding you farther out, or the current could drag you into deeper water when you're not expecting it. Stay shallow and close to the reef's edge and you will be amply rewarded.

12 Japanese Gardens

This dive along the small fringing reef south of Goat Island is a slow-moving drift dive. Though surface conditions can be choppy, underwater conditions are perfect for all skill levels, as the current gradually brings you from the east to the west coast of the island.

Location: South of Goat Island

Depth Range: 3-18m (10-60ft)

Access: Boat

Expertise Rating: Novice

The dive begins in a calm area opposite a long rocky ridge. You'll quickly drop to 12m. There is little point in going any deeper until you reach the rock valley running between a bedrock platform and several large boulders. This valley is about 15m long and 5m wide, and lies at about 15m. From here, the current sweeps you along a steep-sided fringing reef covered in small encrusting corals and sponges, sea fans, sea plumes, giant barrel sponges, tube sponges, hydroids and knobby corals.

All along the reef, various species of damselfish tend to their algal gardens. Be cautious, as they can be quite aggressive if you approach too closely. Large queen angelfish swim in groups of two or three. Look also for

MICHAEL LAWRENCE

Yellow tube sponges predominate on this section of the reef.

snake eels, which forage here even during daylight hours. The most common of the eels in Tobago is the spotted moray—it often pokes its head out of a crevice, opening and closing its mouth in what looks like a threatening behavior, but is really just the moray's way of breathing.

Shooting Mantas

Manta rays (*Manta birostris*) are common around Speyside, especially on most dives around Little Tobago Island. Although a good fish-photography lens like the standard 35mm lens on the Nikonos or Sea & Sea amphibious cameras may be adequate, it's best to use a wide-angle lens. Try the Nikonos 20mm or 15mm lens, the Sea & Sea 16mm or 12mm or, better still, any wide-angle lens wider than 20mm on a housed camera. Wide-angle will allow you to include the entire creature and possibly a diver in the shot. On the down side, a wide-angle lens can make the manta seem small or far away.

The mantas in Tobago are used to divers and will let you come fairly close. They do not tend to shy away from electronic flash, but try not to set your flash off in their eyes as it can impair their vision. Mantas are night-feeders and have very sensitive eyes. A manta may swim very close to you or even rub against you. Under no circumstances should you handle the mantas and never chase them to get your shot. Meet the manta halfway, approaching it slowly and sympathetically, and you will be amply rewarded.

MICHAEL LAWRENCE

Though Tobago's manta rays have grown accustomed to divers, never grab or ride them.

13 Angel Reef

This steeply sloped fringing reef along the west shore of Goat Island is a favorite of many of the area's first-time divers and is popular among experienced divers and photographers as well. The closest coral reef to the Speyside dive shops, Angel Reef offers a safe shallow area entry from the dive boat. Though the reef crest has been damaged by passing storms and by the small fishing boats that anchor there, once you get over the lip of the fringing reef wall, the corals are in much better condition.

Location: West of Goat Island

Depth Range: 3-25m (10-82ft)

Access: Boat

Expertise Rating: Novice

Though Angel Reef has some fine coral and sponge growth and plenty of fish to see by day, this dive is most memorable at night. The sloping wall is riddled with thousands of nooks and crannies where parrotfish ensconce themselves in mucous cocoons for protection while they sleep. There are literally thousands of red night shrimps all over the reef—look for their eyes glowing in your dive light. Spotted spiny lobsters are common, as are the much larger Caribbean spiny lobsters. Giant basket stars are found here with the usual night hunters—spotted scorpionfish, whitespotted soapfish, longspine squirrelfish and plenty of silvery bonnetmouths.

It is also a treat to find long-spined sea urchins, which were wiped out from large areas of the Caribbean by disease several years ago. These urchins play an important part in the living reef's ecology because they feast on the algae that might otherwise smother

and kill the living coral. Be careful not to get poked by the spines, which can easily puncture both neoprene and flesh, causing a painful wound.

During the day, you can continue north along the reef where you will eventually pick up the current again. In this area, look for a massive old anchor embedded in the coral and covered in sponges. This section of the reef should not be visited at night as the reef runs offshore, where the tidal stream is much stronger and the waves higher. These conditions can make it difficult for your dive boat to find you.

LAWSON WOOD
Look for the red night shrimp's eyes glowing in your dive light.

14 Bateaux Reef (Aquamarine)

Known to divers as either Bateaux Reef or Aquamarine, this rocky ridge extends from the shoreline to the Weather Rocks, a set of rocks protruding above the waves. The surge often precludes anyone from diving around the ridge, but when conditions are calm, the many tropical and pelagic fish make it worth diving.

Look for tarpon patrolling the upper water column and large barracuda lower down, hovering along the edge of the rocky slope that drops to 21m. Though the area has sparse coral growth, plentiful plankton flowing through this end of the island promote the growth of a vari-

Location: East of Bateaux Bay

Depth Range: 12-25m (40-82ft)

Access: Boat

Expertise Rating: Advanced

ety of sponges. Apparently, this encourages the fish to breed more often as well, as there are tons of fish fry in the water around this reef throughout the year.

MICHAEL LAWRENCE

15 Sleeper

This dive—near what are known locally as the Black Rocks—is another of those dives that is completely dependent on the weather conditions. Because of the exposure, conditions are too rough for diving more often than not.

Location: North of Little Tobago Island

Depth Range: 12-25m (40-82ft)

Access: Boat

Expertise Rating: Advanced

One side of the rocks has an easy, gentle slope cut with fissures and cracks. The other side is more vertical, with mini-walls encrusted in hydroids, tunicates, small cup corals and iridescent green solitary disc and plate corals. If you plan your dive correctly, you should be able to dive around the rocks, allowing you to see all aspects of the site.

Around the encrusting marine life you will find a huge variety of blennies and gobies. Saddled blennies flit around the rocky ledges, while redlip blennies seem to keep just out of your camera's range. Tiny cleaning gobies and dwarf blennies are also present.

LAWSON WOOD

Queen angelfish are the most colorful fish you'll see in these waters.

Tobago's current-swept waters foster more large sponges than corals.

St. Giles Islands Dive Sites

The north shore of Tobago is incredibly rich in marine life and the St. Giles Islands are a wonderful place to dive. This small group of islands is unique in that it lies at the crossroads of the Caribbean Sea and the Atlantic Ocean. They are often regarded as a mecca for adventure diving, and rightly so. Most dive sites around the islands are subject to oceanic surge, and the Guyana Current pushes through the area at quite a speed. The waters in this area contain vast amounts of plankton and sustain large colonies of giant brain corals. Though the Guyana Current lessens the underwater visibility somewhat, the rewards of diving in this area are very high in terms of pelagic life. Stingrays are common, as are mantas, large tarpon and barracuda. Because of the confluence of the Caribbean and Atlantic, the St. Giles Islands sites tend to have different marine-life communities than other areas of Tobago.

It takes about 20 to 30 minutes to reach the islands by dive boat from either Speyside or Charlotteville. If you approach from Charlotteville, the first landmark dive site you see is London Bridge, a solitary rock southwest of the St. Giles Islands. This rock has a massive natural archway and is the starting point for many different dives.

LAWSON WOOD

Divers can explore the interior of London Bridge's massive natural arch.

St. Giles Islands Dive Sites	Good Snorkeling	Novice	Intermediate	Advanced
16 Sail Rock			●	
17 South St. Giles (St. Giles Drift)	●	●		
18 Marble Island			●	
19 Washaroo			●	
20 Rocky Mountain Low		●		
21 Rocky Mountain High			●	
22 London Bridge				●

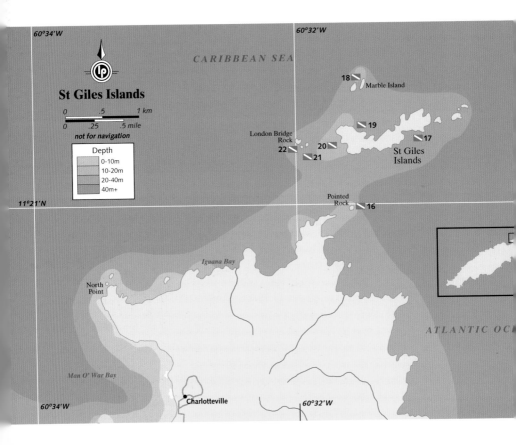

16 | Sail Rock

Sticking up above the water like a sail, this lonely pinnacle is almost midway between northeastern Tobago and the St. Giles Islands. As you dive around the pinnacle, you are likely to get a little boost from the current, but you'll also get some shelter from the numerous rocky spurs. Watch for a natural arch that you can swim through at around 18m.

Location: Near Pointed Rock

Depth Range: 9-20m (30-66ft)

Access: Boat

Expertise Rating: Intermediate

Boulder brain and star corals dominate the area. Fed by the nutrient-rich current, these corals grow to larger-than-average size. One of the delights you should look for is the redspotted hawkfish, the only hawkfish species found in the Caribbean. White and brown vertical bands run down the length of its body and bright reddish spots cover its head, upper body and dorsal fin. It can be quite hard to find as it rests in coral crevices but, if approached slowly with nonthreatening movements, this colorful fish makes a great photographic subject.

Sail Rock is notable for its schooling jacks, Bermuda chub and barracuda. It can be difficult to concentrate on the small marine creatures of the reef when you are preoccupied looking for big fish out in the blue.

LAWSON WOOD

Colonial feather duster worms grow at the base of a sponge.

17 South St. Giles (St. Giles Drift)

The topography at this site consists of some massive rocky boulders and hundreds and thousands of coral domes. South St. Giles is typically performed as a drift dive. It is essential to carry a signaling device (such as a marker tube) to alert the dive boat of your whereabouts when you surface. It is also mandatory to use a surface marker buoy on all drift dives in these waters.

Similar to many of the Speyside dives, the reef slopes rather steeply down to a sandy seabed at around 15m. The slope is dotted with small coral heads and the seabead has small patches of coral-encrusted boulders, healthy hard corals and sea plumes interspersed with sand patches. The seabed is also home to large

Location: South of St. Giles Island

Depth Range: 6-15m (20-50ft)

Access: Boat

Expertise Rating: Novice

schools of snappers, and grunts, flounders and stingrays.

This end of the island experiences a strong current. Expect to see packs of rainbow runners and large crevalle jack. Tarpon, kingfish and spadefish are also common. Divers often hear the clicks and whistles of passing dolphins, though underwater encounters are very rare.

18 Marble Island

Marble Island is actually made up of two distinct rock formations, which lie just north of the St. Giles Islands. These lonely outcrops are regularly pummeled by both the Atlantic swell and the Caribbean surge, as the two mighty bodies of water converge at this point. It is no surprise that this area is navigable only when conditions are perfectly calm.

The dive is done in the surge channel between the rock formations. The channel's maximum depth ranges from 21m at the north end to 10m at the south end closest to the St. Giles Islands. At 21m you'll find a small arch formed by three large boulders—you can swim through the archway when there is no tidal surge.

Fed by the current, marine life is profuse. Look for large pelagics like spotted eagle rays and hawksbill turtles, which are attracted to the rich feeding opportuni-

Location: Marble Island

Depth Range: 12-25m (40-82ft)

Access: Boat

Expertise Rating: Intermediate

ties. These roaming pelagics like the large jellyfish that appear here occasionally.

The rock sides are very steep—nearly vertical in places—and drop well beyond 30m. Sessile life is sparse until you get below 20m, when the corals give way to large deepwater gorgonian sea fans, large branching hydroids in a variety of colors, and hundreds of Christmas tree worms. Fish life is profuse—you're likely to see large parrotfish, hogfish, rainbow runners and snapper.

LAWSON WOOD

The nutrient-rich currents around the St. Giles Islands foster notably large barrel sponges.

19 Washaroo

This exposed site along the north coast of the St. Giles Islands is often rendered undiveable by the massive surge that pounds this stretch of coast. On the rare days when conditions are favorable, divers will be rewarded with abundant marine life.

Location: North of St. Giles Islands

Depth Range: 12-21m (40-70ft)

Access: Boat

Expertise Rating: Intermediate

Washaroo is the local name for the midnight parrotfish. This and other parrotfish species hang around the site's

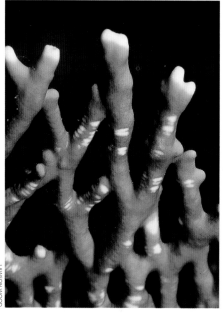

LAWSON WOOD

This fire coral bears teeth marks from parrotfish.

rocky ridges and boulders, which are covered in healthy sponges and small hard corals. All over the large coral field you can see the distinctive teeth marks of parrotfish on the coral, indicating where the fish have used their fused "beaks" to scrape away at the living polyps. Lobsters, crabs, squirrelfish, bigeye snapper and cardinalfish lurk in the nooks and crannies, as does the occasional nurse shark.

The fish are not especially shy and can be approached easily. The area's juvenile French angelfish seem particularly mesmerized by camera flashes. The juvenile's bold black and yellow stripes are different from the adult's coloration, which is gray with yellow-rimmed scales. Tiger groupers are commonly seen, some of which grow to over a meter long. A variety of colorful hamlets—small members of the sea bass family—are also found in the area.

20 Rocky Mountain Low

Large sea plumes, sea fans and rocky coral mounds line the west and southwest shores of the St. Giles Islands. In this topographical setting, Rocky Mountain Low offers divers an opportunity to observe a variety of colorful and photogenic marine life. The visibility is often poor in this area due to the mas-

Location: West of St. Giles Islands

Depth Range: 2-20m (7-66ft)

Access: Boat

Expertise Rating: Novice

sive amounts of plankton that pass through on the tidal stream, but the area has huge aggregations of large brain corals, sea fans and tons of invertebrates.

It is hard to miss the numerous branching anemones, found in the nooks and crannies of the reef. Their colors range from brown to gray to turquoise, with fine white lines leading to their branching tips. Be careful when taking close-up photos of these creatures, as their tentacles are covered with stinging nematocysts. Photography is doubly difficult because this anemone species is sensitive to movement and will rapidly retract its tentacles from view if dis-

turbed. Spotted cleaner shrimp usually associate with the branching anemone and are always a delight to find.

Also common is the juvenile spotted drum, often observed doing its underwater dance. Drums are constantly in motion, gyrating and swimming in circles, darting into cover and then out into the open again. Found underneath coral ledges, these tiny fish are distinctively marked by large vertical black bands that extend along a huge dorsal fin and tail. Large numbers of parrotfish and wrasse forage under dead corals and along the algal beds that cover the rocky ledges. You may even be able to find an elusive toadfish on this dive.

Little Angels

The coloring of the juvenile French angelfish is completely different than that of the adult. The juvenile has a similar shape (though smaller, of course) but is completely black with five vertical bright yellow stripes. As the fish matures, the stripes fade and gold crescents emerge on the edges of the scales. The juvenile French angelfish is easily confused with the juvenile gray angelfish as they have similar coloring. To tell them apart, look closely at their tails. The French (both adult and juvenile) has a rounded tail, while the gray has a square-cut tail. Also, the French juvenile's tail is black with yellow markings around its oval border. The gray juvenile has yellow bar on its foretail and is white or transparent along the very end.

Juvenile French angelfish.

Mature French angelfish.

21 Rocky Mountain High

This dive is along a section of the St. Giles Islands' southwest fringing reef that extends far out from shore toward London Bridge Rock. You'll start in 10m over a healthy coral patch, and drop down to a sandy channel where divers regularly encounter huge roughtail stingrays.

Location: West of St. Giles Islands

Depth Range: 10-21m (33-70ft)

Access: Boat

Expertise Rating: Intermediate

A large roughtail stingray rests on the sand.

As you travel west toward London Bridge, the terrain changes to a series of massive stone blocks separated by narrow channels. The blocks host only sparse coral growth but are heavily encrusted with hydroids, small cup corals, colorful sponges and bryozoans. Angelfish and butterflyfish are common and appear in their lifelong mating pairs. It is always a delight to see the juveniles that often accompany them.

Turn back toward the St. Giles Islands after you pass the blocks, as the current will often begin to pick up. Though London Bridge is nearby, it is best undertaken as an entirely separate dive.

22 London Bridge

Named for its resemblance to the famous masonry bridge immortalized in the children's rhyme, this massive natural arch breaks the surface of the water. The site's awesome above-water majesty continues below, but the site should only be dived when conditions are calm. Divers will enjoy exploring the deep and narrow passageway running through the center of London Bridge.

The dive is normally started at 15m on the north side of the arch. A long rocky ridge to the east funnels the water through the archway and the current will

Location: Near London Bridge Rock

Depth Range: 2-20m (7-66ft)

Access: Boat

Expertise Rating: Advanced

push you gently through a cleft in the rock. Be especially careful here as the opening is only 1m wide, though it gradually expands to about 3m wide. You'll enter the passageway at 15m and ascend to the more sheltered exit at 9m. As much of the dive is in deep shadow, it is best to bring a dive light to illuminate the colorful sponges and tunicates lining the rocky walls.

The sides of the main archway are deeply pitted by coral organisms. Peeking into the shaded areas will reveal cup corals and translucent sponges, such as the yellow calcareous sponge and spiny ball sponge. Fish are everywhere—small groupers wait for prey while schools of tiny silversides play in and out of the shadows, trying to avoid harassment by jacks and trumpetfish.

Near the exit of the archway, two large boulders rise to within 6m of the surface. Deepwater gorgonians interspersed with large growths of orange elephant ear sponges cover the rock surfaces. You can either end the dive here or, depending on the direction of the current, follow the wall to the west, where it slopes gradually, or to the east and north, where the wall becomes much more vertical in some places. This section of the reef has a variety of encrusting corals, sponges and an abundance of fish.

LAWSON WOOD

Colorful sea fans extend from the inside of London Bridge's rocky arch.

Man O' War Bay Dive Sites

Along Tobago's northeast shore, Man O' War Bay is one of the most sheltered bays on the island. The village of Charlotteville, on the bay's east side, has become popular with visiting cruise ships. You reach Charlotteville after a drive down some very steep and winding roads—as you turn the last corner, the village and bay come as something of a delightful surprise and the view is superb. The bay is surrounded by a rocky shoreline to the west and two separate curves of golden sand to the east. Pirate's Bay, to the northeast, is the largest of the bay's beaches. It tends to be popular with novice divers and its small reef formations are ideal for snorkeling. The large solitary rocks to the south are also popular dive sites for novice and intermediate divers.

LAWSON WOOD

Picturesque Charlotteville, on the shores of Man O' War Bay, is northwest Tobago's main town.

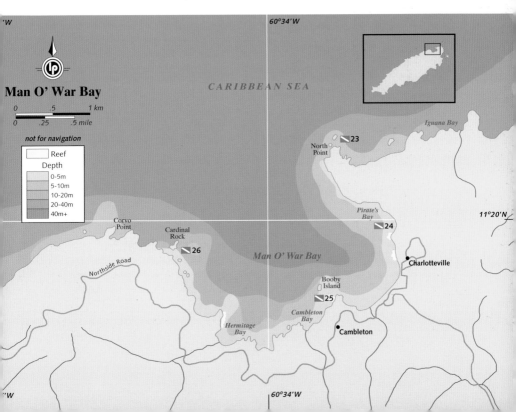

Seagulls congregate on a local fishing boat.

Man O' War Bay Dive Sites	Good Snorkeling	Novice	Intermediate	Advanced
23 Long Rock	●	●		
24 Pirate's Reef	●	●		
25 Booby Island (Big Rock)	●	●		
26 Cardinal Rock	●		●	

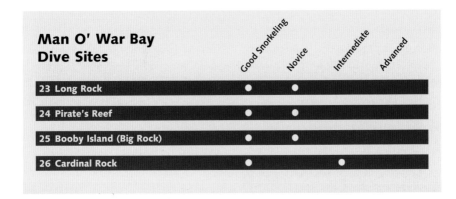

Man O' War Bay

0   .5   1 km
0   .25   .5 mile

not for navigation

Reef
Depth
0-5m
5-10m
10-20m
20-40m
40m+

CARIBBEAN SEA

Iguana Bay

North Point

23

Pirate's Bay

24

11°20'N

Corvo Point

Cardinal Rock

26

Northside Road

Man O' War Bay

Charlotteville

Booby Island

25

Cambleton Bay

Hermitage Bay

Cambleton

60°34'W

23 Long Rock

Just outside Man O' War Bay, northeast of Charlotteville, a long rock breaks the surface of the water, separated from the main part of the island by a deep channel through which all local boat traffic passes. Although this site does not have profuse coral or sponges, it is home to many species of blenny and goby, perhaps more than any other dive site in Tobago. Virtually every nook, cranny, abandoned worm cast, hole and even shell appears to host one of these exotic little fish, which dart around picking morsels of food from the current or working at a cleaning station.

Location: Northeast of Man O' War Bay

Depth Range: 6-9m (20-30ft)

Access: Boat

Expertise Rating: Novice

At cleaning stations you can find predators and their prey peacefully waiting to be stripped of parasites and decaying skin or scales, all enmity forgotten for this brief period of time. Look for bar jacks hanging vertically in the water, their mouths open in a submissive gesture. Parrotfish tend to rest at a 45° angle, while snappers and grunts stay horizontal as they lie in wait for their checkup on the reef. Cleaning stations are a vitally important facet of the marine world.

Groomers of the Sea

STEVE ROSENBERG

A tiger grouper gets a cleaning from an eager pair of gobies.

Observant divers will discover a variety of symbiotic relationships—associations in which two dissimilar organisms participate in a mutually beneficial activity—throughout the marine world. One of the most interesting symbiotic relationships is found at cleaning stations, where one animal advertises its grooming services to potential clients with a series of inviting undulating movements.

Cleaner species include wrasse, shrimp, angelfish, butterflyfish or tang. In Tobago, perhaps most common of all the cleaners is the cleaning goby. These tiny fish have a blue-and-white striped body with a yellow V on their heads. They swarm all over the hard stony corals waiting for fish to approach their protected area of the reef. Once a fish makes the appropriate signals to be cleaned, the gobies enter every available space and clean off any debris, decaying skin or infection. When danger approaches, the fish will close its mouth and gills, but still leave enough room for the gobies to exit the much larger fish and retreat to safety. Although the customer could have an easy snack, it would never swallow the essential cleaner. The large fish benefits from the removal of parasites and dead tissue, while the little cleaner is provided with a "free" meal.

Divers will find that if they approach a cleaning station carefully, they'll get closer to more fish than is normally possible and will observe behavior seen nowhere else on the reef.

24 Pirate's Reef

Pirate's Reef lies opposite the landslide at the north end of Man O' War Bay, west of Charlotteville. Shore access is found at the edge of the beach, before the headland on the right hand side of the bay. The reef extends for 50m off-shore and has a maximum depth of 12 to 15m. It is mainly used for diver training and night dives.

Location: Pirate's Bay

Depth Range: 4-15m (13-50ft)

Access: Boat or shore

Expertise Rating: Novice

The rocky ridge is poor in coral growth, though you will find some elkhorn coral and many small corals. The north end of this bay is a natural fish nursery, where you can find many different species of juvenile angelfish and butterflyfish. Numerous small wrasse abound, and small rays, flounder and gobies can be found on the sandy bottom. At night, the reef comes alive with small spotted lobsters, eel and mollusks.

As this reef is close to shore and in quite shallow water, it is ideal for snorkeling and shallow night diving. The bay in this area is generally calm and sheltered, making the water conditions ideal.

LAWSON WOOD

Elkhorn coral favors shallow waters, like those at Pirate's Reef.

The Pirates of Pirate's Bay

Pirate's Bay derives its name from the secluded haven it provided to marauding buccaneers, who established a base here three centuries ago. The island provided ripe grounds for piracy after rival colonial powers, tired of battling over Tobago, declared it a "no-man's land." As a consequence, Tobago became a staging grounds for pirate attacks on both treasure-laden Spanish ships sailing for South America and British cargo ships in the Grenadines. It's rumored that there's still buried treasure around Pirate's Bay.

Today, this lovely deserted bay is a feeding ground for the frigate bird, a sort of pirate in its own right. The frigate bird feeds itself by attacking terns and gulls in mid-air and snatching their food.

25 Booby Island (Big Rock)

Though Booby Island is used more often by divers in training than by experienced divers, there are many good photo opportunities here. The water is generally clear with visibility around 12m, though this can be better or worse depending on periodic storms from June to November. Though the area is quite shallow and you may find yourself snorkeling more than diving, the subsea topography is scenic and well worth the effort.

The island is surrounded by a rubble plain consisting of large rocks topped with small gorgonian sea fans and lots of fire coral. The rubble area gradually slopes down on the outer seaward side to

Location: Man O' War Bay

Depth Range: 2-25m (7-82ft)

Access: Boat

Expertise Rating: Novice

a sandy plain at 25m where it levels off. Sand gobies, yellowhead jawfish and flounder are common throughout the site, but you'll find most of the marine life on the rubble area. In shallower regions, watch out for huge flat boulders completely covered in fire coral, which has a distinctive yellow color. Look closely at the boulders to find secretary blennies poking their heads out of empty tube worm burrows.

As you proceed toward the southeast side of the island (the side closest to the mainland), you'll find a nice wall that starts at around 9m and rises vertically above the water line. This side of the island consists principally of bedrock topped with fire coral and small hard and soft corals. Look for a couple of gullies, which are generally filled with silverside minnows.

LESLEY ORKSON

A yellowhead jawfish emerges from its burrow.

26 Cardinal Rock

Cardinal Rock is a sheltered site found along the west shore of Man O' War Bay. Though considered a deep dive, most guides start in the shallow area nearest the shore, where you'll find lots of sergeant majors, goatfish and damselfish. From there you will circle toward the deep and, in some places, vertical walls on the pinnacle's seaward side. These walls start above water level and drop rapidly through a series of boulder steps to 42m. Cardinal Rock is close to the outer ocean, so you can expect to see large pelagics such as turtles, eagle rays and big barracuda. Most guides finish the dive by circling back toward the entry point, where there are plenty of interesting fish and invertebrates to see while you wait through your safety stop.

Large sea fans and black corals decorate the rocky slopes, which host the usual attendant parrotfish and large numbers of bluehead wrasse. Like their close relatives the parrotfish, wrasse go through several color phases as they

Location: Western Man O' War Bay

Depth Range: 7-40m (23-130ft)

Access: Boat

Expertise Rating: Intermediate

mature. If there is no adult male within the group, or if the adult male is killed, one of the females will change into a male, who will then be in charge of a harem of the smaller yellow fish. It is only the "super male," in its terminal or adult phase, that has a blue head.

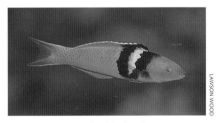

A "super male" bluehead wrasse.

A diver descends a steep portion of wall at Cardinal Rock.

Brightly colored sponges decorate many of Tobago's reefs.

North Coast Dive Sites

The north coast of Tobago, from Man O' War Bay west to Pigeon Point, is dotted with numerous little sandy bays, and fringing reefs extend from every headland. Most of these bays have one or two old anchors still embedded in the reef. This is the sheltered Caribbean side of the island. Protected from the Guyana current, the waters tend to be clearer than in other diving areas on Tobago. It is also less of a spawning ground than the other dive regions, so you'll find fewer juveniles and small fish here.

The north coast, especially the central portion of the north coast, is the least-dived stretch of coastline around the island. There are no dive shops along this part of coast and sites tend to be a long way for the dive boats from other parts of island to travel. The closest dive shops are in Charlotteville (to the northeast) and Pigeon Point (to the southwest), but some of the central bay sites are best accessed from shore. When you can convince an operator to take you here, however, you will be amply rewarded with a variety of sites suitable to all skill levels.

A drive along the north coast brings you past Englishman's Bay and many other scenic areas.

For mapping purposes, we've split the north coast dive sites into two regions: the Central North Coast and the Western North Coast. Along the central north coast, two sets of offshore rocks host advanced dive sites, while several more-sheltered bays offer easier diving and snorkeling sites along the edge of a sandy patch. The western north coast dive sites tend to be more popular and easier to access. They offer more varied terrain, including deep walls, large boulders and caves. Farthest west, you approach the massive Buccoo Reef. This natural barrier reef, which extends north from Pigeon Point, caused the demise of many ships throughout the years.

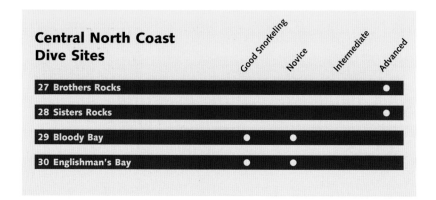

Central North Coast Dive Sites	Good Snorkeling	Novice	Intermediate	Advanced
27 Brothers Rocks				●
28 Sisters Rocks				●
29 Bloody Bay	●	●		
30 Englishman's Bay	●	●		

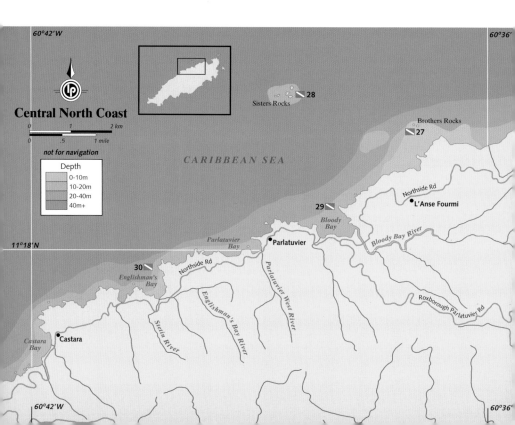

27 Brothers Rocks

The Brothers Rocks lie close to shore, northwest of the town L'Anse Fourmi. Though the rocks are mostly bare of coral growth due to the surge often encountered in the area, the site remains popular with local divers.

Location: Brothers Rocks

Depth Range: 6-40m (20-130ft)

Access: Boat

Expertise Rating: Advanced

The inside shelf closest to shore drops gradually to 8 or 10m, but the outer north and west walls drop rapidly to about 40m. Divers will generally descend along the outer walls to the large boulders at the wall's base, which create hundreds of overhangs, nooks, crannies and small caverns that house a variety of fish and critters. Deepwater gorgonians and black corals are common. Look for huge numbers of yellow tube sponges, barrel sponges and some devil's sea whips in the deeper areas. Schools of jacks and small barracuda are often seen, as are Atlantic spadefish. Lots of cowry shells and other mollusks can be found but, due to the depth of the dive, your time to find them is limited. You will have to come back to see more!

Schooling Atlantic spadefish.

28 Sisters Rocks

Northeast of the Brothers Rocks, the Sisters Rocks are a series of five large pinnacles that rise steeply from the seabed at 36m and are separated by surge channels. Another much smaller pinnacle is found to the west. It is impossible to see all of this large area on just one dive, and perhaps even impossible on a hundred dives. The area is usually split into three distinct dive sites—the Quarry, East Sisters and West Sisters.

Location: 3km (2 miles) north of Bloody Bay

Depth Range: 6-40m (20-130ft)

Access: Boat

Expertise Rating: Advanced

The Quarry is the farthest west of the three sites. Though little of the rock protrudes above the surf, the rock drops in tiers to a sandy base at 36m. The rocky slope's thousands of layers make it a perfect home for moray eels, lobsters and squirrelfish. Also check out the large tunnel found here—it is only negotiable when conditions are favorable, without a ground swell or tidal surge.

East Sisters is usually done as an easy drift dive. At about 21m, you'll find horizontal ledges all around the cliff wall. This is an excellent place to spot bigeye snappers and banded coral shrimps which are everywhere. The first 7m below the water, though dive-able, are subject to massive surge and invariably rough seas. These shallower portions of the pinnacles tend to be fairly devoid of life other than some encrusting corals and sponges, but they do manage to attract large numbers of wrasse and parrotfish. Deeper down, you'll find plenty of tropical fish, snapper and various grouper species. Jacks form small schools around the rocks and hunt the silversides that arrive during the summer months.

The **West Sisters** group consists of two large rocks. This dive brings you quite deep, as the rocks drop steeply from 15m to a sandy seabed at around 40m. The terrain here is similar to the other dives in this area, with hundreds of nooks and crannies where you'll find lobsters and eels. The coral is sparse until you get below 25m, where large groups of gorgonian sea fans and devil's sea whips stretch their long thin stalks up into the current. If you look closely, you may get lucky and find the wire coral shrimp, a tiny shrimp that lives on the sea whips and is considered very rare in the Caribbean. Stingrays are common along the seabed.

South of Sisters Rocks are three sunken rock pinnacles and a 10m-long tunnel at around 20 to 23m. Though easily negotiated, the tunnel is a bit dark, as a bend at the end of the shaft obscures the exit. Nurse sharks are common near the tunnel as are large moray eels, chromis, damselfish and creole wrasse.

LAWSON WOOD

Submarine boulders are covered in corals.

29 Bloody Bay

During the June to November rainy season, mud and runoff from the mountains can cause poor visibility in Bloody Bay, but this problem occurs primarily by the river entrance and improves after a couple of clear days. Because of the high levels of fresh water, corals here are stunted in size and are generally low and encrusting, though the coral quality improves at the bay's outer edges.

Location: Bloody Bay

Depth Range: 6-12m (20-40ft)

Access: Boat or shore

Expertise Rating: Novice

It is uncommon to find dive operators visiting this site, because it's a long trek by dive boat. Some boat operators will come here upon request, but most divers and snorkelers enter from the shore. Access is easy down the sloping sandy beach to the water's edge. The bay is quite sheltered and mostly free of boat traffic, making it almost perfect for snorkelers.

Along the northern stretch of the bay, look for odd-shaped encrusted lumps—these are remnants of ships destroyed in a particularly bloody sea battle, for which the bay is named. Little is known about this historic battle, though it is thought have been fought between the Dutch, Spanish and English, who vied for colonial control of the island in the 17th and 18th centuries.

Large areas of turtle grass are important fish and invertebrate nurseries. Look closely in the sandy areas near the edges of the turtle grass clumps for red heart urchins half buried in the sand. Also look for cushion sea stars, which scavenge on the sea floor. Stingrays hang out on the sand flats between the rocky reefs—they feed on the area's many small shrimp, mollusks and hermit crabs.

When disturbed, the hermit crab will quickly retreat into its shell.

30 | Englishman's Bay

Englishman's Bay is a fairly easy dive down a gentle slope strewn with boulders and large coral heads. The quality of the coral life improves the deeper you dive. Among the many large strands of sea plumes and sea rods, you'll find slender filefish and trumpetfish, which align themselves to the bend and sway of the sea rods. The boulders have lots of holes and crevices where bigeye snappers and juvenile spotted drums can be found. Look under the ledges for the waving antennae of a banded coral shrimp, the

Location: Englishman's Bay

Depth Range: 9-25m (30-82ft)

Access: Boat

Expertise Rating: Novice

largest of the cleaner shrimps found in the Caribbean.

The bay has excellent snorkeling potential, as its sides are very rugged, providing an ideal habitat for encrusting corals, tunicates and sponges. Silverside minnows are often found in the shallows and the area is well known for large numbers of tropical fish and invertebrates. The area is much more rocky than some of the other bays, so the visibility is generally better year-round.

LAWSON WOOD

Shy trumpetfish lurk among swaying soft corals.

Western North Coast Dive Sites	Good Snorkeling	Novice	Intermediate	Advanced
31 Culloden Bay	●	●		
32 Arnos Vale	●	●		
33 *Maverick (Scarlet Ibis)*				●
34 Mount Irvine Wall	●	●		
35 Buccoo Channel	●	●		
36 Angel Reef	●	●		

31 Culloden Bay

Frequented by both local and visiting divers, Culloden Bay is fairly sheltered and has a varied profile. In a relatively small area you can see everything from ancient coral reef structures to good-quality living corals, an interesting sand plain and even a couple of old ship anchors. As a predominantly shallow site, it is ideal for snorkeling, either from the shore or from a dive boat, which anchors in clear sandy areas, away from the delicate corals.

The area where the coral meets the sand is perhaps the most interesting part of the bay, as the bases of the coral heads have lots of small corkscrew anemones. Look for the usual attendant cleaning shrimp and snapping shrimp. Snapping shrimp can be aggressive toward intruders—their small size is

Location: Culloden Bay

Depth Range: 7-25m (23-82ft)

Access: Boat or shore

Expertise Rating: Novice

certainly not a threat to a diver, but their behavior is interesting to watch.

Yellow goatfish can be found excavating the sand with their adapted chin barbels. Stingrays are also present, as are chain morays, which love this terrain. Large sea plumes dot the reef and host trumpetfish and tiny filefish. Schools of blue chromis and creole wrasse are abundant in the water column. There are more groupers here than at most other sites.

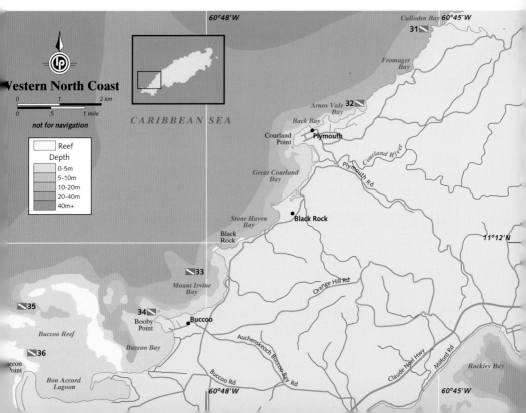

32 Arnos Vale

This sheltered bay, found at the foot of the Arnos Vale Hotel, is excellent for both snorkeling and diving. Traditionally, this bay was dived only rarely, but it has recently become more popular with hotel guests who don't want to travel far. It is a convenient and enjoyable daytime dive and an excellent night dive, when the colors of the reef and encrusted rocks come alive under the illumination of a dive light.

Location: Arnos Vale Bay

Depth Range: 2-20m (7-66ft)

Access: Boat or shore

Expertise Rating: Novice

LAWSON WOOD

A dive light brings out the true colors of the reef.

Divers and snorkelers access the bay via a steep sandy slope, which quickly gives way to large boulders, some of which are gigantic. This spur-and-groove reef virtually encloses the entrance of the bay. A spur-and-groove reef is characterized by raised coral "spurs" separated by wide sandy gullies— it looks something like a hand with the fingers spread apart.

Though lacking good soft-coral growth, the reef hosts some very large brain corals and boulder star corals. The bay is highly regarded as an important fish breeding area, so look for predators like barracudas, triggerfish and jacks. This site always yields schools of Caribbean reef squid, and damselfish can be found on nearly every rock. Also, the many eager sergeant majors at this site have grown accustomed to free handouts from hotel guests.

33 *Maverick (Scarlet Ibis)*

Originally named the *Federal Maple*, then the *Scarlet Ibis*, this former ro-ro (for "roll-on, roll-off") ferry was scuttled by the Tobago Dive Association in May 1997. After a thorough cleanup—all hazardous wastes and oils were removed and hatchways secured for free access through the ship—the ferry was again renamed the *Maverick* and settled on a sandy bottom in 30m. It sits upright and her bow faces due north. It has become a magnet to marine life and is the only dive attraction in an area that would otherwise be a rather featureless sandy plain.

Location: Mount Irvine Bay

Depth Range: 25-30m (82-100ft)

Access: Boat

Expertise Rating: Advanced

Visibility here is normally not great—around 9 to 15m—and as you descend the permanent shot line, you're likely to see hovering clouds of fish before you can make out the ship's structure. This is a great place to watch small silversides, large boga and even larger jacks round smaller fish into tight schools before attacking them in a wonderful display of aquatic acrobatics.

Through the cargo area you can easily access the rear hold, which is completely open. The derrick above the hold is a massive archway of steel covered in small gorgonians, hydroids, encrusting sponges and algae. A resident jewfish hangs out near the forward hatch— it will likely follow you around the entire dive like a puppy. Because it's blind in one eye, it can be approached easily and

makes for some striking photo opportunities.

The *Maverick* is a true oasis where all manner of marine life can be found. However, since this is a deep dive, divers should be sure to check their gauges regularly. It's easy to overstay your welcome on this wonderful wreck while playing tag with the grouper or being stalked by the large barracuda.

The *Maverick's* large resident jewfish befriends a diver.

LAWSON WOOD

34 Mount Irvine Wall

Accessible by shore or by boat, Mount Irvine Wall is an extension of the rocky shoreline southwest of Mount Irvine Bay. This is a perfect site for both divers and snorkelers, as much of the rocky reef lies above the tide line (so it's easy to follow) and it has some protection from the westerly wave surge.

Location: Mount Irvine Bay

Depth Range: 6-12m (20-40ft)

Access: Boat or shore

Expertise Rating: Novice

The wall, which lies in only about 12m, has been smoothed over by centuries of pounding waves. Several gullies, some with algal debris on the bottom, cut their way through the wall. One of the larger gullies has a small archway and cave at the rear where you'll find a school of glassy sweepers. The walls surrounding this cavern are brilliantly colored with bright orange, red and yellow encrusting sponges.

Other than some low encrusting species and a few types of algae, you won't see much hard coral or sponge growth on the exposed outer edges of the wall, but yellow tube sponges are found in more sheltered areas. Literally thousands of Christmas tree worms and clumps of social feather dusters cover the wall. Gobies and blennies are also common, as are wrasse and parrotfish. You may even find the uncommon swollen-claw mantis shrimp wandering over the reef. Deeper down, look for rose lace corals. Venus sea fans look as if they take quite a battering here, but you'll see little flamingo tongue snails on virtually every one. Divers should watch their buoyancy, as there is quite a lot of fire coral in the area.

To the north, inside Mount Irvine Bay, is a dive site known as the **Flying Dutchman**, also sometimes referred to as **Mount Irvine Reef**. The site is named after the 17th-century Dutch East India Company ship that met its demise on the shallow area of the reef. Though almost nothing remains of the ship's main portions, you can find three decrepit cannons and a few bits of coral-encrusted wood on the sea floor. These remnants are the highlight of an otherwise ordinary dive along a low rocky ridge topped by fire corals, small sea fans, cactus corals and numerous sponges.

A lone magnificent feather duster worm.

35 Buccoo Channel

Buccoo Reef became a designated marine park in 1973. Its massive proportions extend north of Bon Accord Lagoon to about 23km offshore, encompassing a circular area several hundred meters in diameter. The sheltered inner lagoon, where the local fishermen keep their boats, is shallow with several deep channels that provide safe access.

Location: Outer Buccoo Reef

Depth Range: 5-15m (16-50ft)

Access: Boat

Expertise Rating: Novice

The Buccoo Channel runs between a pair of steep slopes covered with honeycomb plate corals and sunray lettuce corals. You'll also see both thickly encrusting and hemispherical lettuce corals with lots of ridges and valleys. Look for numerous moray eels, rock beauties, large gray angelfish and banded butterflyfish. Eagle rays and nurse sharks are known to inhabit the channel and, on rare occasions, divers have even encountered manta rays. Though divers and snorkelers should be wary of boat traffic in the channels, traffic tends to be light, so there is little danger involved.

In the past, the shallow waters of the Buccoo Reef spelled disaster for many sailing ships.

36 Angel Reef

This gently sloping dive site on the southwest portion of Buccoo Reef is home to hundreds of different coral species. Lettuce corals, cactus corals, brain corals and star corals predominate, with large stands of sea plumes and rods growing in between them. Thousands of nooks and crannies shelter small moray eels and a host of tropical fish.

Location: Southwestern Buccoo Reef

Depth Range: 2-20m (6-66ft)

Access: Boat

Expertise Rating: Novice

The reef is bordered on either side by wide sandy plains. In stormy weather, sand particles tend to get swept over the reef, so visibility is often poor. Though Angel Reef is usually done as a training dive or the second dive of the day, there is still plenty to satisfy the avid photographer.

LAWSON WOOD

A diver examines an old anchor embedded in the reef.

Columbus Passage Dive Sites

The Columbus Passage between Tobago and Trinidad is often regarded as one of the top drift-diving locations in the Caribbean, but it is only appropriate for experienced divers who are familiar with drift diving procedures. Divers on drift dives should always be accompanied by an experienced divemaster carrying a surface marker buoy. The buoy—which floats on the surface and is attached to the dive guide by a long lightweight rope—is used to indicate the diver's position to the boat tender. Moving with the current, the dive boat captain uses the buoy to monitor and follow the dive group as it progresses over the reefs.

MICHAEL LAWRENCE

Pigeon Point has several fine beaches shaded by palm trees.

Although the coast between Pigeon Point and Crown Point is Tobago's main resort area, there are only a handful of dive sites here. Aside from the offshore drift dives, which take up to 30 minutes to reach by boat, most of the sites are either accessible from shore or are just a short boat ride away.

LAWSON WOOD

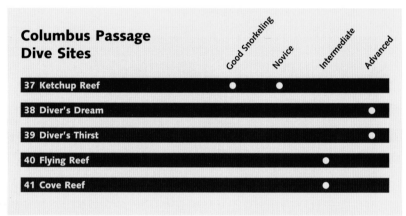

Columbus Passage Dive Sites

	Good Snorkeling	Novice	Intermediate	Advanced
37 Ketchup Reef	●	●		
38 Diver's Dream				●
39 Diver's Thirst				●
40 Flying Reef			●	
41 Cove Reef			●	

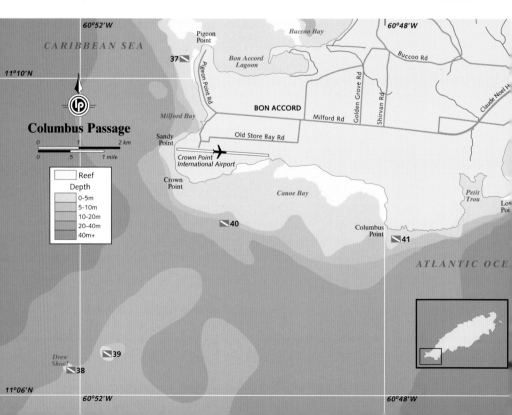

37 | Ketchup Reef

Ketchup Reef is a small reef that skirts the north part of Milford Bay. Because it is a fringing reef (rather than barrier reef like Buccoo Reef), Ketchup Reef is attached to the shoreline, following the contours of the coast. The reef was named after a cargo ship that wrecked here and was full of—you guessed it— ketchup. No evidence remains of the wreck on the seabed, so the reef life is the site's highlight. The maximum depth is about 10 to 12m and it is suitable for all levels of divers.

Reef life is abundant, with many different sea rods, sea plumes, soft corals and hard corals. Fish life is not as profuse as it once was, as the area was heavily depleted by local fishing in the past. Fishing activity has declined significantly in recent years, so you'll find most species of angelfish, butterflyfish,

Location: Southwest of Pigeon Point

Depth Range: 3-12m (10-40ft)

Access: Boat

Expertise Rating: Novice

wrasses, parrotfish, snappers and grunts in the shallows. Dive operators bring their less-experienced clients here as it's close to shore and perfect for snorkeling and training dives.

The site is especially popular for night diving, when snake eels, small spotted lobsters, shrimp and squirrelfish emerge. The colorful reef is illuminated by your dive light and small creatures like the burrowing anemone and the pistol shrimp come out to feed.

LAWSON WOOD

Sharpnose puffers like to play hide-and-seek among the sponges.

38 Diver's Dream

Diver's Dream lies southwest of Crown Point in the shallow reefs around Drew Shoal. It is accessed by a 30-minute boat trip from Pigeon Point. The shallowest part of this dive lies at just 6m. From there, the rocky ridges slope gently down to about 15m. Look for the fracture lines where rocky strata run parallel to the rock peaks. Large boulders and huge misshapen barrel sponges occupy the sandy troughs. Nurse sharks rest in the sand beneath the boulders and rocky ridges. All over the reef, you'll see queen angelfish, often in groups of four or five.

Location: 8km (5 miles) southwest of Crown Point

Depth Range: 6-20m (20-66ft)

Access: Boat

Expertise Rating: Advanced

Perhaps the main attraction of this dive site is the thousands of giant barrel sponges, some of which have grown to more than 2m across. The sponges have been bent and misshapen by the current—in some cases, the sponges' top openings have been squashed flat. Around the barrel sponges are dark volcano sponges, orange elephant ear sponges, large deepwater gorgonian sea fans and feather brush hydroids.

If you enjoy drift diving, this site is a must. The current ranges from one knot to more than three knots—strong enough to push you along with little effort on your part, but usually not so much that you'll lose control. The current makes for quite an exhilarating dive, but its danger should never be underestimated. As with all drift dives in Tobago, divers must always be accompanied by a divemaster with a surface marker buoy and must carry a signaling device in case of an emergency. Divers have been swept away from the group and held under by the current, surfacing hundreds of meters from the dive boat. A signaling device will make it easier for a boat captain to find and retrieve you if you get separated. The local dive shops make every effort to ensure that your dive is as safe as possible. If you are unsure of your expertise level or your ability to safely perform this dive, talk with your dive center before heading out.

LAWSON WOOD

A barrel sponge misshapen by the current.

39 Diver's Thirst

This dive is a little closer to shore than Diver's Dream and is really a continuation of the same reef. However, due to the differing subterranean topography, the current in this area is less forceful than on Diver's Dream.

The dive starts along a bedrock ledge with an undercut crevice along its seaward side. The ridge starts at around 9m and then quickly drops away. Dive over and along the series of raised rocky ridges and sandbars that look almost like petrified waves. On the side of the ridges that is exposed to the current, low scrubby corals, deepwater sea fans, sponges, hydroids and algae predominate. On the sheltered side, you'll find tube sponges, lobsters, moray eels and damselfish. As at Diver's Dream, expect to dive around thousands of huge barrel sponges, all bent at 45° angles by the force of the prevailing current. Nurse sharks are seen on virtually every dive

Location: 6km (4 miles) southwest of Crown Point

Depth Range: 9-25m (30-82ft)

Access: Boat

Expertise Rating: Advanced

and blacktip reef sharks are spotted frequently.

The current will sweep you gradually into deeper water, and before long you will find yourself at 25m, so be extra careful to watch your depth gauge. Because of the almost constant tidal stream, underwater visibility is generally around 15 to 25m. During the winter rainy season, the Orinoco river wash will sometimes reach this far north and the area is best avoided, as the underwater visibility may drop to nil.

On drift dives, your divemaster will be attached to a surface marker buoy.

40 Flying Reef

This is another drift dive with a strong current. It's only 2km from the shore opposite the runway for the Crown Point International Airport, in the western portion of Canoe Bay. The current pushes you westward and, although the reef is quite shallow, you can expect to see good quality corals and sponges along its length. Over the centuries, a number of natural channels have been carved through the reef by the prevailing current. There are large sea fans, plumes and rods to examine—though you'll hardly get a chance, as the current keeps you constantly on the move.

Large numbers of parrotfish are found throughout the region—queen parrotfish are common and you might even

Location: Opposite the Crown Point airport runway

Depth Range: 7-20m (23-66ft)

Access: Boat

Expertise Rating: Intermediate

spot a rainbow parrotfish, which is the largest of the species. Also look for creole wrasse, blue chromis and schools of small southern sennet. In the sandy channels, predators lie in wait for small fish fry. Even flying gurnards, always seen in their lifelong mating pairs, can be found around the reef.

Large schools of southern sennet are common at Flying Reef.

41 Cove Reef

A continuation of Flying Reef, Cove Reef lies along the southern shoreline that stretches east from Crown Point. The reef resembles a larger and deeper version of Buccoo Reef, with a steep slope riddled with interesting nooks and crannies that host all manner of marine life. The combination of living and dead corals creates a curious underwater terrain.

Location: Southeast of Columbus Point

Depth Range: 2-20m (7-66ft)

Access: Boat

Expertise Rating: Intermediate

A huge variety of corals and sponges inhabits these waters and you'll see thousands of fish everywhere. Parrotfish and wrasse are common, as are several species of moray eel. There are many balloonfish—although they can grow quite large, most of the balloonfish here are no more than 24cm long. The reef is dotted with the usual congregation of gobies, blennies and cleaning stations. In some areas, the corals form large overhangs and small caves where you'll find large lobsters and bigeye snappers.

The currents have twisted these barrel sponges into unusual shapes.

Worldwide, little is known about diving in Trinidad—in fact, many people would say that there is no diving in Trinidad at all. Though international divers do not often visit the area, adventurous visitors encounter an astonishing variety of marine life around the offshore islands. What makes Trinidad's diving different from Tobago's is primarily its poorer underwater visibility. Trinidadan waters are tainted a greenish-brown by the floodwaters of the Orinoco as well as runoff from Trinidad's major rivers, particularly during the rainy season from June to November. On a good day, the visibility may be as much as 15m (50ft), but on a bad day may be as low as 2m (6ft).

Here you can find large schools of queen angelfish, hundreds of Atlantic spadefish, schooling hammerheads and giant manta rays, as well as rare sea fans found elsewhere in the Caribbean only in very deep water. Rare cup corals and virtually every species of blenny are commonly found in this area. Overhanging rocks are home to curiously shaped sponges. A thermocline at 15m (50ft) opens up visibility, giving you glimpses of rare deepwater corals.

Trinidad's diving is based mainly around the Bocas Islands west of Chaguaramas in the channel between Trinidad and Venezuela, and the group of islands southeast of Point Gourd. Sheltered from the muddy river wash of the Orinoco, dive sites along the north coast host better coral life.

Trinidad's north coast is lined with beautiful bay beaches.

Predictably, the diving industry in Trinidad is not particularly well established. There are just two diving operators in Chaguaramas, but only one has full facilities for visiting divers, including gear sales and rentals, air, a dive boat and instruction.

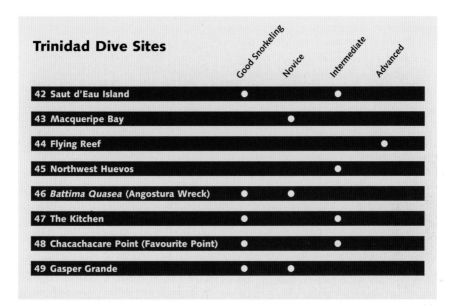

Trinidad Dive Sites	Good Snorkeling	Novice	Intermediate	Advanced
42 Saut d'Eau Island		●	●	
43 Macqueripe Bay		●		
44 Flying Reef				●
45 Northwest Huevos			●	
46 *Battima Quasea* (Angostura Wreck)	●	●		
47 The Kitchen	●		●	
48 Chacachacare Point (Favourite Point)	●		●	
49 Gasper Grande	●	●		

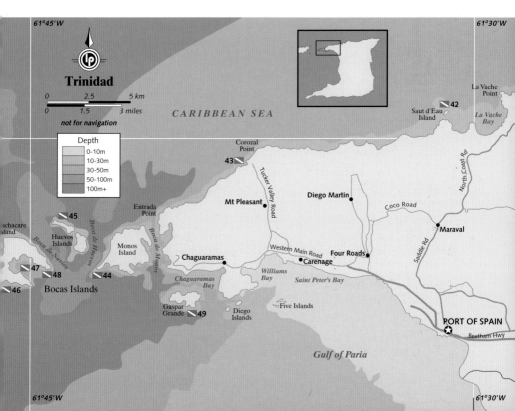

42 Saut d'Eau Island

Saut d'Eau Island is north of the headland between Saint Cite Bay and La Vache Bay, west of La Vache Point. This large rocky outcropping is covered in scrubby vegetation and cacti that grow surprisingly close to the water's edge and well within the splash zone. Much of the Trinidadan north coast escapes the bulk of the Orinoco floodwaters, so the water surrounding the island is

Location: Around Saut d'Eau Island

Depth Range: 6-18m (20-60ft)

Access: Boat

Expertise Rating: Intermediate

LAWSON WOOD

Saut d'Eau Island lies just off the north shore.

quite clear and there is little fresh water in the mix, which helps in coral growth. A large fringing reef made up of good quality hard and soft corals rings Saut d'Eau. Much of the boulder slope has small encrusting corals and sponges that support a huge variety of fish life. Look for the many species of blenny and goby, as well as the usual Caribbean species of parrotfish, angelfish, butterflyfish, wrasses, groupers and snappers.

43 Macqueripe Bay

This popular dive is also known commonly as **Stingray Stretch** because of the large number of roughtail and southern stingrays that frequently visit. Look for them around the edge of the sandy area where the rocky boulder slope bottoms out at around 9m. If you move slowly, you can approach the stingrays quite closely. They tend to rest on the seabed during the day and forage for mollusks and other sub-sand dwellers only at dusk and at night.

Though there are few good hard corals, the encrusting sponges are colorful and prolific and the site is dotted with zoanthids and cup corals. Tobaccofish can be found around the boulders. Large

Location: Macqueripe Bay

Depth Range: 6-12m (20-40ft)

Access: Boat or shore

Expertise Rating: Novice

queen angelfish and rock beauties are also found at this site. As you travel farther out into the bay, you'll see large boulders covered in soft corals. Expect to see big schools of jackfish and king mackerel. In this area you will usually hear dolphins vocalizing underwater, and divers recently got an unusual treat when they spotted a rare albino dolphin in the bay.

This site can be accessed from the shore but is mainly dived by boat. The best shore access is from the edge of the bay, where the rocky ridge meets the sea. Conditions have to be near-perfect to dive from the shore, as the surge and waves can be quite dangerous in a northerly swell.

A spiny lobster cautiously explores a reef in Macqueripe Bay.

44 Flying Reef

Flying Reef is off Point Courant on the southwest coast of Monos Island. Monos is the first of the Bocas Islands, which extend from Trinidad's northwest coast and form the northern border of the Gulf of Paria. This site is a favorite of local divemasters who praise its quality and variety of fish life, including groupers, snappers, grunts, parrotfish and all the tropicals. Divers sometimes spot dolphins passing through on their way from Venezuela. This dive site is a must for any underwater photographer.

Flying Reef consists of a long rocky spur that juts out from islands at a max-

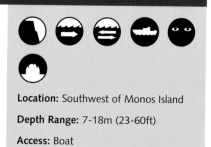

Location: Southwest of Monos Island

Depth Range: 7-18m (23-60ft)

Access: Boat

Expertise Rating: Advanced

imum depth of 18m. You'll dive along this spur amid small encrusting pencil corals, sea whips and colorful sea rods. Look for huge sea fans, along with other hard and soft corals. The reef slopes up to 9m and the dive ends at 18m in a calm bay behind the reef.

The currents can get quite strong as you approach the channel between Monos and the Huevos Islands. Also be careful, as the visibility may be drastically reduced. Fortunately, the strong current keeps mud from gathering on the reef, so the corals are continuously fed with plankton and are healthier than in other areas.

Nurse sharks sleep under rocky ledges during the day and emerge to hunt at night.

45 Northwest Huevos

The current gets stronger as you approach Northwest Huevos from the sheltered marinas at Chaguaramas. The coastline is deeply sculpted by the pounding Atlantic surge and there is little hard coral growth because of the high levels of fresh water and suspended particulate brought in by the Orinoco. That said, look for nice sea fans on all the lower

Location: Northwest of Huevos Islands

Depth Range: 7-18m (23-60ft)

Access: Boat

Expertise Rating: Intermediate

slopes and thousands of tiny cup corals, which grow singly and in small colonies.

Caverns, crevices and large surge gullies characterize this end of the island. Box crabs—known locally as "shame-faced crabs" because of their habit of burying themselves up to their eyes in the sand—inhabit areas near the boulders along the seabed. Look for balloonfish and porkfish. Large jewfish are often found in the caves and schools of jacks are also common.

A small balloonfish explores a reef bed.

46 *Battima Quasea* (Angostura Wreck)

This wreck lies well broken-up in about 6m in Chacachacare Island's southern bay, opposite the dried-up salt pans where islanders used to collect sea salt. The wreck site is named after the ship's cargo of Angostura bitters, a traditional liqueur and stomach cure made only on Trinidad.

Location: South of Chacachacare Island

Depth Range: 2-7m (6-23ft)

Access: Boat

Expertise Rating: Novice

The island is in direct line of the Orinoco freshwater run-off, which washes through the Gulf of Paria. As a result, there is very little coral growth and the water color is a light brown, like tea. On the plus side, the water is several degrees warmer than around Tobago and there is a massive amount of fish life. In particular, the site is a haven for juvenile fish. This wreck dive is an easy introduction to Trinidad diving and divers should not be put off by the water color or seeming lack of visibility.

The ship's wooden timbers are covered in an algal fuzz and host tiny blennies, especially spinyhead and sailfin blennies, in virtually every hole. The sailfin blenny's territorial behavior is comical—watch as it lifts itself out of its protective burrow, extends its sail-like fin and attacks its neighboring blennies. Juvenile French angelfish swim around and under the ship's timbers, while sharpnosed pufferfish poke around the algae looking for small crustaceans.

Angostura Bitters

The Angostura company produces Trinidad's best-selling local rums, but is perhaps better known internationally for its bitters, a liqueur with an old-fashioned label that is found in medicine cabinets and barrooms worldwide. The recipe for the bittersweet libation, which is made only in Trinidad, is shrouded in mystery—only seven people know the true mixture. The concoction was originally invented in 1824 by Dr. J.B.G. Siegert, a young German surgeon who had traveled to South America to join Simon Bolívar's Venezuelan liberation army. As a practicing physician, Siegert sought a tonic for the myriad stomach disorders that plagued troops fighting

jungle warfare. Now solely produced in Trinidad by Siegert's direct descendants, the bitters are famous around the world not only as a stomachic, but as a mix for cocktails.

47 The Kitchen

This dive site lies offshore from the ruins of the kitchens of what was once a large leper colony. The settlement, which occupied the shores around Chacachacare Bay until the mid-1970s, had all the modern conveniences. You can still see the doctor's house, small villas, theater, laundry and hospital, all completely abandoned. Many of the roads are overgrown and, sadly, the buildings have fallen prey to vandals, but the bay is beautiful and hosts great diving within its sheltered confines.

Underwater, a boulder slope falls away quickly. Because the area is bathed in a silty mixture of fresh and salt water, the sea fans—such as the carmine sea spray and the rigid red telesto—are striking in color. Tiny cup corals cover most of the crevices and small hydroids and encrusting sponges are everywhere.

Location: Chacachacare Bay

Depth Range: 6-20m (20-66ft)

Access: Boat

Expertise Rating: Intermediate

These waters host all of the brightly colored tropicals common to the Caribbean, including schools of queen angelfish—an unusual sight, as queen angelfish are normally solitary or found in mated pairs. Caverns formed by tumbled boulders yield moray eels, lobsters and giant crabs. There is a thermocline at around 15m—below this level the water is colder and has a different salinity, changing the nature of the species of sea fans and sponges you'll see.

The sheltered confines of Chacachacare Bay are a favored stopover for visiting yachts.

48 Chacachacare Point (Favourite Point)

Southeast of the island, this site ranges from the sheltered inner bay to the current-swept channel separating Chacachacare and the Huevos Islands. The boulder slope descends well below the safe diving range and divers will experience a notable thermocline below 15m. If you only have a thin wetsuit, you may be uncomfortable diving in the colder water. Below 15m, the water becomes notably darker as well—it is akin to diving at dusk, so bring along your dive light.

The fish life on this corner is profuse, with large schools of porkfish, Caesar grunt and Bermuda chub. All of the

Location: off Chacachacare Point

Depth Range: 5-20m (16-66ft)

Access: Boat

Expertise Rating: Intermediate

Caribbean angelfish species are found in this area and a truly remarkable range of blennies and gobies occupies every corner, nook and cranny. Huge balloonfish hide under boulder overhangs, which are festooned with little, pale-white cup corals and hydroids. You'll see many large sea fans and literally thousands of fish. The corals at this site are much more profuse than at any other site in the Bocas Islands and, although the ever-present current can be a bother, it is well worth the effort.

Look for rare red sea fans at Chacachacare Pt.

Blennies peek out of every nook and cranny.

49 Gasper Grande

Regarded mainly as a training dive, the Gasper Grande site is along an easy rocky ridge that runs south from the island to a sandy seabed. The seabed is dotted with boulders and turtle grass patches, which shelter hundreds of variegated sea urchins. Commonly called "sea eggs," these sea urchins are sometimes harvested for their edible roe. Green razorfish are also common in the area—look in particular for the juvenile, which blends in amazingly well with the surrounding algae. There is little large coral growth at this site due to the high content of silty fresh water, but the rocky slopes are covered in small sponges, brilliantly colored sea fans and literally thousands of tiny cup corals.

West of the island, you'll find a number of caverns extending into the island. Although these caverns have not yet been fully explored, experts do not believe they are linked with the on-land Gasparee Cave system. Curious visitors can tour the on-land caves, which are filled with stalactite and stalagmite formations.

Location: Southwest of Gasper Grande Island

Depth Range: 2-15m (7-50ft)

Access: Boat

Expertise Rating: Novice

A yellowprow goby rests on the seabed.

The area's low viz makes photography difficult.

Marine Life

Situated at the confluence of the Caribbean Sea and the Atlantic Ocean, Trinidad and Tobago host a fairly typical representation of Caribbean marine life. Though not as diverse as some parts of the Caribbean, most Caribbean species are recorded here, often in very large numbers. You will also see some species from the colder Atlantic waters, which are pushed into the area by the Guyana Current. The current

LAWSON WOOD

fosters a massive planktonic food chain, which is responsible for certain anomalies, such as unusually large brain corals, sea fans and barrel sponges; schooling queen angelfish; and regular encounters with mantas and giant stingrays. Because of the low visibility in some spots, you will find shade-loving black corals and whip corals at unusually shallow depths, sometimes at less than 9m (30ft).

Common names are used freely but are notoriously inaccurate and inconsistent. The two-part scientific name, usually shown in italics, is more precise. It consists of a genus name followed by a species name. A genus is a group of closely related species that share common features. A species is a recognizable group within a genus whose members are capable of interbreeding.

Common Invertebrates

branching anemone
Lebrunia danae

giant basket star
Astrophyton muricatum

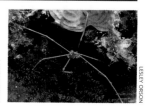

arrow crab
Stenorhynchus seticornis

fingerprint cyphoma
Cyphoma signatum

magnificent feather duster worm
Sabellastarte magnifica

moon jellyfish
Aurelia aurita

Caribbean reef octopus
Octopus briareus

golden coral shrimp
Stenopus scutellatus

spotted cleaner shrimp
Periclemenes yucatanicus

lettuce sea slug
Tridachia crispata

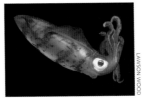

Caribbean reef squid
Sepioteuthis sepioidea

painted tunicate
Clavelina picta

Common Vertebrates

queen angelfish
Holacanthus ciliaris

balloonfish
Diodon holocanthus

saddled blenny
Malacoctenus triangulatus

secretary blenny
Acanthemblemaria maria

longsnout butterflyfish
Chaetodon aculeatus

spotfin butterflyfish
Chaetodon ocellatus

blue chromis
Chromis cyanea

sharptail eel
Myrichthys breviceps

spotted moray eel
Gymnothorax moringa

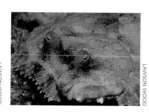

slender filefish
Monacanthus tuckeri

peacock flounder
Bothus lunatus

yellowprow goby
Gobiosoma xanthiprora

golden hamlet
Hypoplectrus gummigutta

hogfish
Lachnolaimus maximus

black jack
Caranx lugubris

sharpnosed puffer
Canthigaster rostrata

manta ray
Manta birostris

grey snapper
Lutjanus griseus

blackbar soldierfish
Myripristis jacobus

squirrelfish
Holocentrus adscensionis

tarpon
Megalops atlanticus

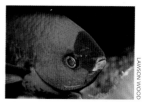

smooth trunkfish
Lactophrys triqueter

bluehead wrasse
Thalassoma bifasciatum

creole wrasse
Clepticus parrae

Hazardous Marine Life

Marine animals almost never attack divers, but many have defensive and offensive weaponry that can be triggered if they feel threatened or annoyed. The ability to recognize hazardous creatures is a valuable asset in avoiding accident and injury. The following are some of the potentially hazardous creatures most commonly found in Trinidad and Tobago.

Bristle Worm

Also called fire worms, bristle worms can be found on most reefs. They have segmented bodies covered with either tufts or bundles of sensory hairs that extend in tiny, sharp, detachable bristles. If you touch one, the tiny stinging bristles lodge in your skin and cause a burning sensation that may be followed by a red spot or welt. Remove embedded bristles with adhesive tape, rubber cement or a commercial facial peel. Apply a decontaminant such' as vinegar, rubbing alcohol or dilute ammonia.

Fire Coral

Although often mistaken for stony coral, fire coral is a hydroid colony that secretes a hard, calcareous skeleton. Fire coral grows in many different shapes, often encrusting or taking the form of a variety of reef structures. It is usually identifiable by its tan, mustard or brown color and finger-like columns with whitish tips. The entire colony is covered by tiny pores and fine, hair-like projections nearly invisible to the unaided eye. Fire coral "stings" by discharging small, specialized cells called nematocysts. Contact causes a burning sensation that lasts for several min-

utes and may produce red welts on the skin. Do not rub the area, as you will only spread the stinging particles. Cortisone cream can reduce the inflammation and anti-histamine cream is a good painkiller. Serious stings should be treated by a doctor.

Portuguese Man-o-War

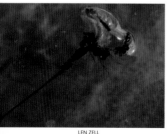

This colonial organism, distantly related to the jellyfish, is found at the surface, and is recognizable by its purplish, translucent "floats" and long, trailing tentacles. Its tentacles, which can reach 50ft (15m) or more in length, are armed with exceedingly toxic stinging cells, which can cause a painful sting. Beached man-o-wars are still hazardous, even weeks after they've dried out and appear dead. Sting symptoms range from a mild itch to intense pain, blistering, skin discoloration, shock, breathing difficulties and even unconsciousness. If stung, apply a decontaminant such as vinegar, papain or dilute ammonia and seek immediate medical aid. Allergic reactions can be severe and life-threatening.

Moray Eel

Distinguished by their long, thick, snake-like bodies and tapered heads, moray eels come in a variety of colors and patterns. Don't feed them or put your hand in a dark hole—eels have the unfortunate combination of sharp teeth and poor eyesight, and will bite if they feel threatened. If you are bitten, don't try to pull your hand away suddenly—the teeth slant backward and are extraordinarily sharp. Let the eel release it and then surface slowly. Treat with antiseptics, anti-tetanus and antibiotics.

Scorpionfish

Scorpionfish are well-camouflaged creatures that have poisonous spines along their dorsal fins. They are often difficult to spot since they typically rest quietly on the bottom or near coral, looking more like rocks. Practice good buoyancy control and watch where you put your hands. Scorpionfish wounds can be excruciating. To treat a puncture, wash the wound and immerse it in nonscalding hot water for 30 to 90 minutes. Administer pain medications if necessary.

Sea Urchin

Sea urchins tend to live in shallow areas near shore and come out of their shelters at night. They vary in coloration and size, with spines ranging from short and blunt

to long and needle-sharp. The spines are the urchin's most dangerous weapon, easily able to penetrate neoprene wetsuits, booties and gloves. Treat minor punctures by extracting the spines and immersing in nonscalding hot water. More serious injuries require medical attention.

LAWSON WOOD

Shark

Sharks come in many shapes and sizes. They are most recognizable by their triangular dorsal fin. Though many species are shy, there are occasional attacks. About 25 species worldwide are considered dangerous to humans. Sharks generally will not attack unless provoked, so don't taunt, tease or feed them. Avoid spearfishing, carrying fish baits or mimicking a wounded fish and your likelihood of being attacked will greatly diminish. Face and quietly watch any shark that is acting aggressively and be prepared to push it away with camera, knife or tank. If someone is bitten by a shark, stop the bleeding, reassure the patient, treat for shock and seek immediate medical aid.

Stingray

Identified by its diamond-shaped body and wide "wings," the stingray has one or two venomous spines at the base of its tail. Stingrays like shallow waters and tend to rest on silty or sandy bottoms, often burying themselves in the sand. Often only the eyes, gill slits and tail are visible. These creatures are harmless unless you sit or step on them. Though injuries are uncommon, wounds are always extremely painful, and often deep and infective. Immerse wound in nonscalding hot water, administer pain medications and seek medical aid.

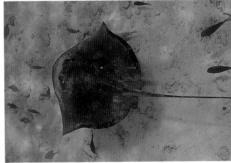

LAWSON WOOD

Touch-Me-Not Sponge

They may be beautiful, but sponges can pack a powerful punch with fine spicules

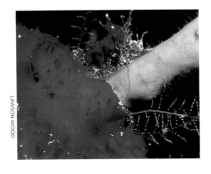

LAWSON WOOD

that sting on contact, even after they've washed up on shore. Red sponges often carry the most potent sting, although they are not the only culprits. If you touch a stinging sponge, do not rub the area. Remove visible spicules with tweezers, adhesive tape, rubber cement or a commercial facial peel. Soak in vinegar for 10 to 15 minutes. The pain usually goes away within a day. Cortisone cream can help.

Diving Conservation & Awareness

MICHAEL LAWRENCE

With the oldest protected rainforest in the world on Tobago, as well as a variety of bird and other wildlife sanctuaries, the islands' terrestrial conservation is much further ahead than its marine conservation. There are designated marine conservation areas on both Trinidad and Tobago, but neither island has instituted any active management to enforce protective regulations. In this area, the principal threats to the marine environment are overfishing and indiscriminate anchoring, which damages the fragile reef life. The newer hotels have their own sewage treatment plants, but in some coastal towns, raw sewage still runs directly into the sea. Be wary of any pipe you see running out to sea, as it is certainly a sewage pipe.

The Institute of Marine Affairs, a governmental organization supported by the Association of Dive Operators, actively spearheads marine-conservation policies on both Trinidad and Tobago. In Trinidad, protected sites are planned around Chaguaramas Peninsula and the Bocas Islands in the northwest, and Salybia Reef in the northeast. Planned protected areas in Tobago include the Buccoo Reef and areas around Little Tobago Island, Goat Island, the St. Giles Islands, Speyside and Man O' War Bay. At the time of print there were still no fully protected marine nature reserves.

Responsible Diving

Dive sites tend to be located where the reefs and walls display the most beautiful corals and sponges. It only takes a moment—an inadvertently placed hand or knee, or a careless brush or kick with a fin—to destroy this fragile, living part of our delicate ecosystem. By following certain basic guidelines while diving, you can help preserve the ecology and beauty of the reefs:

1. Never drop boat anchors onto a coral reef and take care not to ground boats on coral. Encourage dive operators and regulatory bodies in their efforts to establish permanent moorings at appropriate dive sites.

2. Practice and maintain proper buoyancy control and avoid over-weighting. Be aware that buoyancy can change over the period of an extended trip. Initially you may breathe harder and need more weighting; a few days later you may breathe more easily and need less weight. Tip: Use your weight belt and tank position to maintain a horizontal position–raise them to elevate your feet, lower them to elevate your upper body. Also be careful about buoyancy loss: as you go deeper, your wetsuit compresses, as does the air in your BC.

WOLF WINTER

Resist the temptation to collect marine souvenirs—leave shells for others to enjoy as well.

3. Avoid touching living marine organisms with your body and equipment. Polyps can be damaged by even the gentlest contact. Never stand on or touch living coral. The use of gloves is no longer recommended: gloves make it too easy to hold on to the reef. The abrasion caused by gloves may be even more damaging to the reef than your hands are. If you must hold on to the reef, touch only exposed rock or dead coral.

4. Take great care in underwater caves. Spend as little time within them as possible, as your air bubbles can damage fragile organisms. Divers should take turns inspecting the interiors of small caves or under ledges to lessen the chances of damaging contact.

5. Be conscious of your fins. Even without contact, the surge from heavy fin strokes near the reef can do damage. Avoid full-leg kicks when diving close to the bottom and when leaving a photo scene. When you inadvertently kick something, stop kicking! It seems obvious, but some divers either panic or are totally oblivious when they bump something. When treading water in shallow reef areas, take care not to kick up clouds of sand. Settling sand can smother the delicate reef organisms.

6. Secure gauges, computer consoles and the octopus regulator so they're not dangling—they are like miniature wrecking balls to a reef.

7. When swimming in strong currents, be extra careful about leg kicks and handholds.

8. Photographers should take extra precautions, as cameras and equipment affect buoyancy. Changing f-stops, framing a subject and maintaining position for a photo often conspire to prohibit the ideal "no-touch" approach on a reef. When you must use "holdfasts," choose them intelligently (i.e., use one finger only for leverage off an area of dead coral).

9. Resist the temptation to collect or buy coral or shells. Aside from the ecological damage, taking home marine souvenirs depletes the beauty of a site and spoils other divers' enjoyment.

10. Ensure that you take home all your trash and any litter you may find as well. Plastics in particular pose a serious threat to marine life.

11. Resist the temptation to feed fish. You may disturb their normal eating habits, encourage aggressive behavior or feed them food that is detrimental to their health.

12. Minimize your disturbance of marine animals. Don't ride on the backs of turtles or manta rays, as this can cause them great anxiety.

Marine Conservation Organizations

Coral reefs and oceans are facing unprecedented environmental pressures. The following groups are actively involved in promoting responsible diving practices, publicizing environmental marine threats and lobbying for better policies.

Local Organization
Crusoe Reef Society
☎ 628-2207

International Organizations

CORAL: The Coral Reef Alliance
☎ 510-848-0110
www.coral.org

Project AWARE Foundation
☎ 714-540-0251
www.projectaware.org

Coral Forest
☎ 415-788-REEF
www.blacktop.com/coralforest

ReefKeeper International
☎ 305-358-4600
www.reefkeeper.org

Cousteau Society
☎ 757-523-9335
www.cousteau.org

Listings

Telephone Calls

To call Trinidad & Tobago from the U.S. and Canada or from another part of the Caribbean, dial 1 + 868 + the local seven-digit number. From elsewhere, dial your country's international access code + 868 + the local number.

Accommodations

The following hotels are considered diver-friendly because they have dive shops on the premises or nearby. The major international hotels have extra facilities, including some of the islands' most popular restaurants, while the self-catered condos come equipped with kitchens. A full list of hotels, guest houses, cottages and condos is available from the tourist office.

Tobago

Inexpensive

Ian Lambie Guest House
(2 rooms)
Stonehaven Bay, Black Rock
☎ 639-0286

Jetway Holiday Resorts
(9 condos)
Crown Point
☎ 639-8504

Store Bay Holiday Resort
(15 rooms)
Store Bay
☎ 639-8810
Kitchen in each room

Wood's Castle
(9 rooms)
Milford Rd., Bon Accord
☎ 639-0803
Restaurant, bar

Moderate

Blue Waters Inn
(38 rooms)
Bateaux Bay, Speyside
☎ 660-4341
Restaurant, beachfront
Affiliated Diving Service: Aquamarine Dive

Footprints Eco Resort
(9 rooms)
Culloden Bay
☎ 660-0118
Set in nature reserve

Moderate (continued)

Kariwak Village
(24 rooms)
Crown Point
☎ 639-8442
Restaurant, pool

Manta Lodge Resort
(22 rooms)
Windward Rd., Speyside
☎ 660-5268
Restaurant, pool, beachfront
Affiliated Diving Service: Tobago Dive
Experience

Expensive

Arnos Vale Hotel
(38 rooms)
Plymouth
☎ 639-2881
Restaurant, pool, beachfront

Paradise Villas Resort
(10 condos)
Grafton Estate, Black Rock
☎ 639-9556
Pool at each condo

Crown Point Beach Hotel
(77 condos)
Crown Point
☎ 639-8781
Restaurant, pool, beachfront

Rex Turtle Beach Hotel
(125 rooms)
Courland Bay
☎ 639-2851
Restaurant, pool, beachfront
Affiliated Diving Service: Tobago Dive
Experience

Grafton Beach Resort
(108 rooms)
Stonehaven Bay, Black Rock
☎ 639-0191
Restaurant, beachfront
Affiliated Diving Service: Aquamarine Dive

Trinidad

Inexpensive

The Abercromby Inn
(17 rooms)
101 Abercromby St., Port of Spain
☎ 623-5259

Par-May-La's Inn
(11 rooms)
53 Picton St., Port of Spain
☎ 628-2008

The Bight
(10 rooms)
Lot 5, Western Main Rd., Chaguaramas
☎ 634-4389
Restaurant, bar

Moderate

Bel Air International Airport Hotel
(56 rooms)
Piarco International Airport, Piarco
☎ 669-4771
Restaurant, bar, pool

Laguna Mar
(10 rooms)
Paria Main Rd., Blanchisseuse
☎ 628-3731
Restaurant

Expensive

Asa Wright Nature Centre & Lodge
(24 rooms)
Blanchisseuse Rd., Arima
☎ 667-4655
Restaurant; set in nature reserve

Trinidad Maracas Bay Hotel
(36 rooms)
Bay Rd., Maracas Bay
☎ 669-1914
Restaurant, beachfront

Kapok Hotel
(71 rooms)
16-18 Cotton Hill, St. Clair
☎ 622-6441
Restaurant, lounge, pool, spa

Trinidad Hilton & Conference Centre
(394 rooms)
Lady Young Rd., Port of Spain
☎ 624-3111
Restaurants, pool

Diving Services

The following is a complete list of all diving services on both islands. On Tobago, most diving services can run trips to any of part of the island, either through an affliation with a hotel in the area or by transporting small dive boats across the island using a large four-wheel drive. Overland travel to more remote areas is, of course, weather-dependent. Trinidad's diving services are limited.

Tobago

Aquamarine Dive
Speyside
P.O. Box 402, Scarborough
☎ 660-4341 fax: 639-4416
Le Grande, Black Rock
☎ 639-8729 fax: 639-0030
amdtobago@trinidad.net
Sales: Full **Rentals:** Full
Air: Yes
Credit cards: Most major credit cards accepted
Boats: 3 uncovered pirogue-style boats
Trips: All Tobago regions
Courses: Beginner to instructor; specialities
Other: Small branch at Grafton Beach Resort

Derek Chung's Undersea Tobago
P.O. Box 1105, Canaan
☎ 639-7759 fax: 639-4122
Sales: Limited **Rentals:** Full, including cameras
Air: Yes
Credit cards: Visa and Mastercard
Boats: 1 covered pirogue-style boat
Trips: All Tobago regions
Courses: Beginner to assistant instructor; specialities

Tobago (continued)

Dive Tobago Ltd.
Pigeon Point Resort, Pigeon Point
☎/fax: 639-0202
Sales: Limited **Rentals:** Full
Air: Yes
Credit cards: Visa and Mastercard
Boats: 4 uncovered pirogue-style boats
Trips: All Tobago regions
Courses: Beginner to assistant instructor;
specialities

Man Friday Diving
Windward Rd., Charlotteville
☎/fax: 660-4676
mfdiving@tstt.net.tt
Sales: None **Rentals:** Full
Air: Yes
Credit cards: Visa and Mastercard
Boats: 1 uncovered pirogue-style boat
Trips: St. Giles Islands, especially Sister
Rocks
Courses: Beginner to assistant instructor;
specialities

Manta Dive Center Ltd.
Pigeon Point Rd., Pigeon Point
P.O. Box 1090, Canaan
☎ 639-9969 fax: 639-9209
mantaray@ttst.net.tt
Sales: Full **Rentals:** Full
Air: Yes
Credit Cards: Visa and Mastercard
Boats: 2 uncovered pirogue-style boats;
1 covered dive boat
Trips: All Tobago regions
Courses: Beginner to assistant instructor

Proscuba Dive Center
Rovanell's Resort, Store Bay Local Rd.,
Bon Accord
☎/fax: 639-7424
proscuba@tstt.net.tt
Sales: Limited **Rentals:** Full
Air: Yes
Credit cards: Visa and Mastercard
Boats: 1 covered dive boat

Trips: All Tobago regions
Courses: Beginner to assistant instructor;
specialities

R & Sea Divers Den
Spence's Terrace, Milford Rd., Crown Point
☎/fax: 639-8120
rsdivers@tstt.net.tt
Sales: Limited **Rentals:** Full
Air: Yes
Credit cards: Visa and Mastercard
Boats: 2 uncovered pirogue-style boats
Trips: Columbus Channel, especially
Diver's Dream and Diver's Thirst
Courses: Beginner to assistant instructor;
specialities

Scuba Adventure Safari
Milford Rd., Bon Accord
☎/fax: 660-7333
info@divetobago.com
Sales: Full **Rentals:** Full
Air: Yes
Credit cards: Visa and Mastercard
Boats: 2 uncovered pirogue-style boats
Trips: Columbus Channel and Crown
Point area
Courses: Beginner to assistant instructor;
specialities

Sublime Scuba
P.O. Box 1116, Canaan
☎ 639-9642 fax: 639-9386
sublime@tstt.net.tt
Sales: Limited **Rentals:** Full
Air: Yes
Credit cards: Visa and Mastercard
Boats: 1 pirogue-style boat
Trips: Western North Coast and Columbus
Passage
Courses: Beginner to assistant instructor;
specialities

Tobago (continued)

Tobago Dive Experience
Black Rock
Turtle Beach Hotel, P.O. Box 115, Scarborough
☎ 639-7034 fax: 639-7845
Manta Lodge Resort, Speyside
☎ 660-4888 fax: 660-5030
manta@trinidad.net
Sales: Limited **Rentals:** Full
Air: Yes
Credit cards: All major credit cards accepted
Boats: 4 pirogue-style boats
Trips: All Tobago regions
Courses: Beginner to assistant instructor; specialities
Other: Branch at Rex Turtle Beach Resort

Tobago Divemasters
Speyside
P.O. Box 351, Scarborough
☎/fax: 639-4697 or 660-5924
sensei@trinidad.net

Sales: None **Rentals:** Full
Air: Yes
Credit cards: Visa and Mastercard
Boats: 2 pirogue-style boats
Trips: Speyside and St. Giles Islands
Courses: Beginner to assistant instructor; specialities

Wild Turtle Dive Safari
Pigeon Point Resort, Pigeon Point
P.O. Box 154, Scarborough
☎/fax: 639-7936
info@wildturtledive.com
Sales: Limited **Rentals:** Full
Air: Yes
Credit cards: Visa and Mastercard
Boats: 1 pirogue-style boat
Trips: Columbus Passage
Courses: Beginner to assistant instructor; specialities

Trinidad

Dive Specialist Center
The Cove at Chaguaramas Bay
P.O. Box 3123, Carenage
☎/fax: 628-4524
Sales: Limited **Rentals:** Limited
Air: On-site fills
Credit cards: Visa and Mastercard
Boats: 1 pirogue-style boat
Comments: Gulf of Paria and Bocas Islands
Courses: Beginner to assistant instructor; specialities

Rick's Dive World
P.O. Box 573, Port of Spain
☎/fax: 628-1913
rick@wow.net
Sales: Limited **Rentals:** Full
Air: On-site fills
Credit Cards: Visa and Mastercard
Boats: 1 covered dive boat
Trips: Bocas Islands and northern Trinidad
Courses: Beginner to assistant instructor; specialities

Film Processing

Though Trinidad and Tobago both have plenty of film processing shops, only the following four processors can handle E6 slide film processing on site. There is no E6 processing available on Tobago.

Film Processors
143 Tragarete Rd., Port of Spain
☎ 628-3901

Harriman's
9 Chacon St., Port of Spain
☎ 625-4571

Photo House Studio and Lab Ltd.
15 Woodford St., Arima
☎ 667-1684

Photo World
Long Circular Mall, St. James
☎ 622-8567

Tourist Offices

You can find helpful staff and all the glossy brochures you can carry at any of several branches of the Tourism and Industrial Development Company of Trinidad & Tobago (TIDCO), the local tourist board.

Trinidad

TIDCO Main Office
10-14 Phillips St., Port of Spain
☎ 623-1932 fax: 623-3848
www.visittnt.com
tourism-info@tidco.co.tt

TIDCO
Piarco International Airport, Piarco
☎ 669-5196

Tobago

TIDCO
Unit 12, TIDCO Mall, Sangster's Hill, Scarborough
☎ 639-4333 fax: 639-4514

TIDCO
Crown Point International Airport, Bon Accord
☎ 639-8256

Index

dive sites covered in this book appear in **bold** type

Lonely Planet Pisces Books

The **Diving & Snorkeling** guides cover top destinations worldwide. Beautifully illustrated with full-color photos throughout, the series explores the best diving and snorkeling areas and prepares divers for what to expect when they get there. Each site is described in detail, with information on suggested ability levels, depth, visibility and, of course, marine life. There's basic topside information as well for each destination.

Also check out dive guides to:

Australia: Southeast Coast	Cocos Island	Palau	St. Maarten, Saba,
Bahamas: Family Islands & Grand Bahama	Curaçao	Puerto Rico	& St. Eustatius
	Fiji	Red Sea	Texas
Bahamas: Nassau & New Providence	Florida Keys	Roatan & Honduras' Bay Islands	Truk Lagoon
	Jamaica		Turks & Caicos
Bali & the Komodo Region	Northern California & Monterey Peninsula	Scotland	U.S. Virgin Islands
Bonaire		Seychelles	Vanuatu
British Virgin Islands	Pacific Northwest	Southern California	

Lonely Planet Series Descriptions

Lonely Planet **travel guides** explore a destination in depth with options to suit a range of budgets. With reliable, practical advice on getting around, restaurants and accommodations, these easy-to-use guides also include detailed maps, color photographs, extensive background material and coverage of sites both on and off the beaten track.

For budget travelers **shoestring guides** are the best single source of travel information covering an entire continent or large region. Written by experienced travelers these 'tried and true' classics offer reliable, first-hand advice on transportation, restaurants and accommodations, and insider tips for avoiding bureaucratic confusion and stretching money as far as possible.

City guides cover many of the world's great cities with full-color photographs throughout, front and back cover gatefold maps, and information for every traveler's budget and style. With information for business travelers, all the best places to eat and shop and itinerary suggestions for long and short-term visitors, city guides are a complete package.

Lonely Planet **phrasebooks** have essential words and phrases to help travelers communicate with the locals. With color tabs for quick reference, an extensive vocabulary, use of local scripts and easy-to-follow pronunciation instructions, these handy, pocket-sized language guides cover most situations a traveler is likely to encounter.

Lonely Planet **walking guides** cover some of the world's most exciting trails. With detailed route descriptions including degrees of difficulty and best times to go, reliable maps and extensive background information, these guides are an invaluable resource for both independent hikers and those in organized groups.

Lonely Planet **travel atlases** are thoroughly researched and fact-checked by the guidebook authors to ensure they complement the books. The handy format means none of the holes, wrinkles, tears or constant folding and refolding of flat maps. They include background information in five languages.

Journeys is a new series of travel literature that captures the spirit of a place, illuminates a culture, recounts an adventure and introduces a fascinating way of life. Written by a diverse group of writers, they are tales to read while on the road or at home in your favorite armchair.

Entertaining, independent and adventurous, Lonely Planet **videos** encourage the same approach to travel as the guidebooks. Currently broadcast throughout the world, this award-winning series features all original footage and music.

Lonely Planet Online

Get the latest travel information before you leave or while you're on the road

Whether you've just begun planning your next trip, or you're chasing down specific info on currency regulations or visa requirements, check out Lonely Planet Online for up-to-the-minute travel information.

As well as travel profiles of your favorite destinations (including maps and photos), you'll find current reports from our researchers and other travelers, updates on health and visas, travel advisories, and discussion of the ecological and political issues you need to be aware of as you travel.

There's also an online travelers' forum where you can share your experience of life on the road, meet travel companions and ask other travelers for their recommendations and advice. We also have plenty of links to other online sites useful to independent travelers.

And of course we have a complete and up-to-date list of all Lonely Planet travel products including guides, phrasebooks, atlases, Journeys and videos and a simple online ordering facility if you can't find the book you want elsewhere.

www.lonelyplanet.com or AOL keyword: lp

Travel news goes off faster than a bag of prawns in the sun.

Lonely Planet's new monthly email newsletter, **Comet**, brings you the latest travel news, destination ideas, travel tips, health advice, travellers' yarns, raging debates and competitions. All this, and it's free.

To subscribe just enter your email at:
http://www.lonelyplanet.com/comet/

Lonely Planet Publications

Australia
P.O. Box 617, Hawthorn, Victoria 3122
☎ (03) 9819 1877 fax: (03) 9819 6459
email: talk2us@lonelyplanet.com.au

USA
150 Linden Street
Oakland, California 94607
☎ (510) 893 8555, (800) 275 8555
fax: (510) 893 8563
email: info@lonelyplanet.com

UK
10a Spring Place,
London NW5 3BH
☎ (0171) 428 4800 fax: (0171) 428 4828
email: go@lonelyplanet.co.uk

France
1 rue du Dahomey
75011 Paris
☎ 01 55 25 33 00 fax: 01 55 25 33 01
email: bip@lonelyplanet.fr

www.lonelyplanet.com